How to Win Every Argument

An Introduction to Critical Thinking

Nicholas Capaldi

MJF BOOKS
NEW YORK

Published by MJF Books
Fine Communications
Two Lincoln Square
60 West 66th Street
New York, NY 10023

How To Win Every Argument
Library of Congress Catalog Card Number 99-70062
ISBN 1-56731-330-2

This book was originally published by Prometheus Books as
The Art of Deception.

Manufactured in the United States of America on acid-free paper

MJF Books and the MJF colophon are trademarks of Fine Creative Media, Inc.

10 9 8 7 6 5 4 3 2 1

Acknowledgments for the New Revised Edition

I wish to thank Lawrence L. Heintz, University of Hawaii at Hilo, for calling to my attention some difficulties with the rules for determining validity. Special thanks are due to Professor John Greenwood, University of North Carolina at Greensville, for sharing with me his discussion in manuscript form of causation with regard to human action.

Contents

8

10   Contents

Preface

Critical thinking is something that we all do, but we are not necessarily self-conscious about it. Just as we learn to speak our native language long before we learn its grammar, so, too, we think critically long before we realize that this activity also has a structure. And just as those who become self-conscious of the structure of our language also become more effective at communication, so, too, those who become self-conscious of the structure behind critical thinking become more adept in reading comprehension, in exposing the logic of an argument, and in skillfully challenging defective arguments when they are confronted.

In this volume I have tried to explain in a simple and clear fashion the principles behind our critical thinking. With due regard to cultural and historical factors, I have explained what the ideal structure of an argument is, how that ideal becomes a paradigm for critical thinking, and the various ways in which arguments can fail to exemplify that ideal structure. I have provided some guidance on how to use language cues in identifying an argument and its structure. At many points I show how a wide variety of devices, both formal and informal, can be used to buttress arguments and to call attention to their weaknesses.

Critical thinking involves at least two sub-categories. First, to think critically is to think logically. Second, to think critically is to know where and how to challenge the arguments that one comes across in daily life. With regard to logic, I note that it has become a technical discipline and, as such, has tended to focus on the structure of arguments in other technical disciplines, such as mathematics. I have endeavored to keep technical terminology to a minimum and to introduce students only to that part of logic that is routinely needed for everyday purposes, including academic purposes. Rather than discuss informal fallacies in a vacuum or dwell on technical minutia, I have stressed the practical contexts in which such fallacies are likely to appear.

With regard to teaching students how to challenge arguments in a constructive and rewarding way so as to deepen comprehension, I have employed a novel device. In addition to presenting an organized approach to the subject, I have written this book from the point of view of one who wishes to deceive, mislead, or manipulate others. On the assumption that "it takes one to know one," I have found that people are able to detect the misuse or abuse of logic if they themselves are masters of the art of deception. The reader should ask himself how different the world would be if everyone knew—really knew—how to use and thereby how to detect the misuse of logic.

Even after completing the standard course in informal logic, most students are as incapable of spotting a fallacy as they were before they enrolled. A key factor in this failure to teach students to deal with fallacies in real life is the emphasis upon recognition. Typically, the student or reader is asked to identify fallacies in the writings of others, and although he or she must respond, the response is within a primarily passive situation. This narrow textbook approach necessitates that the author or teacher rely upon singularly obvious or simple-minded examples. The transfer to other contexts is rarely made.

In my own experience as a teacher I have found that using a format of active manipulation rather than passive recognition is much more successful. I hope that you, too, will find this approach more rewarding and successful.

Nicholas Capaldi

One

Introduction

WHAT IS LOGIC?

Sometimes the best way in which to explain something is to tell what that something is not. Logic is best explained by presenting examples of what is not logic. Consider the three following cases of the absence of logic.

First, there is an old routine popularized by the famous American comedy team of Abbott and Costello. Imagine that both men are in a radio studio in New York City. Abbott claims that he can prove to Costello that Costello is not there! On the face of it, Abbott's claim appears paradoxical, if not ridiculous, since it is clear to Costello, and to everyone in the audience, that Costello is there. Nevertheless, Abbott persists in his claim. To begin with, Abbott gets Costello to admit that he, Costello, is not in San Francisco. Next, Costello admits that he is not in Chicago. Finally, Costello admits that since he is not in San Francisco and he is not in Chicago, then he must be somewhere else. Abbott then concludes that since Costello is somewhere else, it follows that Costello cannot be in New York City.

Everyone finds the above classic routine amusing. Some of us, however, suspect that there is a trick in Abbott's claim and in his procedure. The question is how to unmask the trick. One way in which the procedure may be contested is to point out that the expression "somewhere else" is never used in a vacuum or in a contextless way. We always use the expression by specifying a frame of reference. Thus, it is silly to talk about someone being "somewhere else" because there is no such place as "somewhere else." "Somewhere else" means either not here, where "here" is specifically or implicitly defined, or it means somewhere other than the place or places explicitly mentioned. In the example given, San Francisco and Chicago are the only places explicitly mentioned. Costello is somewhere other than San Francisco and Chicago. This admission would in no way imply that Costello is not in New York City.

Abbott was not the first person to abuse language, nor are we the first to suggest a rule for using the expression "somewhere else." In fact, there might not even be a rule in any explicit sense until we are forced to examine a troublesome case. Most of us learn to use our language long before we are taught any rules about it. Rules may even be nothing more than explicit formulations of current practice, a formulation forced upon us by someone's discovery of a trick that can be played in the absence of a strict rule.

Second, let us consider an example from philosophy. In Plato's dialogue the *Protagoras,* Socrates questions Protagoras about the relationship between "wisdom" and "self-control." Protagoras asserts that there is no necessary tie between "wisdom" and "self-control." Socrates then raises a long series of questions in answer to which Protagoras asserts three things: that "wisdom" is the opposite of folly; that every word having an opposite has one and only one opposite; and that folly is the opposite of "self-control." Socrates then interrupts Protagoras and offers the following challenge. If "wisdom" is the opposite of folly, and if "self-control" is the opposite of folly, then "wisdom" and "self-control" are two opposites to the same word, namely, folly. However, Protagoras has also admitted that every word having an opposite has one and only one opposite. Either Protagoras must reject the assertion that every word that has an opposite has just one opposite or he must reject his initial assertion that there is no necessary tie between "wisdom" and "self-control." If both of these words, "wisdom" and "self-control," have the same opposite, then they must be synonymous or have the same meaning. Protagoras ends up rejecting his original statement that "wisdom" and "self-control" have no necessary tie.

The foregoing example is interesting for two reasons. First, it shows how it is possible for a relatively intelligent person to think that he understands the meaning of isolated statements and then to recognize the conflict in those statements when someone else brings them together. Second, one of the two conflicting statements is a formulation of a classical logical rule, namely the *law of the excluded middle*. This law states that every statement is either true or false. The assertion that every word having an opposite has one and ony one opposite says essentially the same thing. Protagoras' immediate acceptance of this statement and his rejection of his original statement (i.e., that "wisdom" and "self-control" are not closely related) seems to show that certain rules have a special status. He was much more willing to save the rule than to save his definitions of "wisdom" and "self-control" once he was aware of the conflict.

Third, let us consider an example from contemporary political debate. Consider the following argument.

(1) Communists support unilateral nuclear disarmament.

(2) Liberals support unilaterial nuclear disarmament.

(3) Therefore, Liberals are Communists.

Most of us would agree that statements (1) and (2) are true but that statement (3) is false. But the above argument seems to imply that if statements (1) and (2) are true then statement (3) must be true. Since this argument is puzzling, let us schematize it and then analyze its content. We shall adopt the following symbols:

"C" stands for Communists

"L" stands for Liberals

"V" stands for "supports unilateral nuclear disarmament."

In schematic form the argument now looks like this:

> (1) C is V
>
> (2) L is V
>
> (3) L is C

In order to test the acceptability of the above argument, we now construct another argument with the same schematic form.

> (1) All camels are vegetarians.
>
> (2) Lambs are vegetarians.
> _____
>
> (3) Therefore, lambs are camels.

In schematic form the argument is identical to the argument in the previous paragraph.

> (1) C is V
>
> (2) L is V
>
> (3) L is C

Since most of us would agree that this argument is unacceptable, and since this argument is identical in form to the previous argument, we must also find the previous argument unacceptable.

The importance of the political example is that it shows us how convenient it would be to invent a symbolic technique by which we could test the acceptability of arguments. Moreover, it leads us to raise important questions about our entire discussion. What does it mean to find an argument acceptable or unacceptable? What is an argument? Finally, why are we so concerned to identify acceptable and unacceptable arguments? These questions are best answered in reverse order.

The great significance of logic as a tool for distinguishing acceptable from unacceptable arguments comes in the area of practical affairs. As is evident from the third example, people discuss the most important affairs in life by the use of arguments. Important decisions affecting our lives and our well-being are often presented in the form of arguments. It is precisely because our language is related to our actions that the distinction between acceptable and unacceptable arguments becomes important.

WHAT IS AN ARGUMENT?

Before we can define an argument, we must first consider some more general features of the structure of our language. The smallest unit of our language is the *letter*, and in the English language there are twenty-six letters from "a" to "z." Letters constitute the building blocks out of which the rest of our language is constructed. The next larger unit is the *word*. Words are constructed out of letters, and the construction is done on the basis of rules. The rules for combining letters into words are called *spelling* rules. The next larger unit can be variously called the *clause,* the *sentence,* or the *statement.* Sentences are constructed out of words, and this construction is also carried out on the basis of rules. The rules for combining words into sentences are called rules of *grammar.*

Sentences are usually divided into four types: declarative, exclamatory, imperative, and interrogative. Some logicians have tried to argue that there is a correlation between the type of sentence and the function of the sentence. For example, it is usually argued that declarative sentences convey information or facts and are thus true or false; and it is argued that imperative sentences express commands and are thus not true or false. However, a closer examination reveals that one type of sentence can be substituted for another without necessarily changing the function. For example, I can say "Close the door" (which is an imperative sentence), or I can say "I want the door closed" (which is a declarative sentence).

It is when we have arrived at this level of language that we realize just how complicated the structure of our language is. If we could discuss language simply in terms of the relationships among symbols (what is referred to as *syntax*), then it would be a simple matter to lay out the logic or structure of our thought and langauge. However, in addition to syntax, we must also consider the relationship of symbols to things or objects in the world (what is called *semantics*) and the relationship of language to the user of the language (what is called *pragmatics*). Here it is no easy matter to say what the rules or structures are without getting into deep philosophical debate.

The same problem can be seen in the next larger unit of language after the sentence, namely, the *paragraph*. There are no unambiguous rules for combining sentences into parargraphs. We are usually advised that there is some kind of unity or coherence to sentences in a paragraph, often identified by reference to a topic sentence. But this is not easy to see on purely structural grounds.

There are, on the other hand, certain combinations of sentences or clauses or statements that do have an obvious unity. One combination is called an argument. An *argument* is a group of statements (sentences, clauses), either within one larger sentence or within a group of grammatically distinct sentences, such that one or more of the statements are said to "support," "prove," or "provide evidence for" one other statement. The statement that is supported, proven, or for which evidence is provided is called the *conclusion*. There is one and only one conclusion for each argument. There may be any number of supporting statements. The statements that provide support, offer proof, or provide evidence are called *premises*.

The clue to recognizing an argument is the conclusion: one conclusion, one argument. It should also be noted that the terms "premise" and "conclusion" are relative. That is, the same statement may be both a premise in one argument and a conclusion to another argument. This is because we can have a series of interlocked arguments. In the next chapter I shall discuss clues for identifying arguments.

The classic paradigm of an argument is:

Premise 1:   All men are mortal.
Premise 2:   Socrates is a man.

Conclusion: Socrates is mortal.

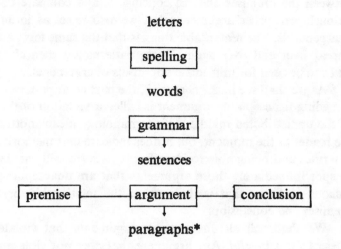

TABLE 1
Elements of Language

letters

↓

spelling

↓

words

↓

grammar

↓

sentences

↓

| premise |—————| argument |—————| conclusion |

↓

paragraphs*

*Only some paragraphs contain arguments.

WHEN IS AN ARGUMENT ACCEPTABLE?

We have now arrived at the question "How do we tell the difference between an acceptable and an unacceptable argument?" If an argument is composed of premises and a conclusion, then one of the differences between an acceptable argument and an unacceptable argument must lie in the relationship between the premises and the conclusion.

One kind of argument is intuitively unacceptable, i.e, an argument that allows us to arrive at a false conclusion from true premises. An example we have already used fits this pattern.

Premise 1: All Communists vote for unilateral nuclear disarmament.

Premise 2: All Liberals vote for unilateral nuclear disarmament.

Conclusion: All Liberals are Communists.

The premises are true but the conclusion is false. Logicians can now proceed to diagram this argument, analyze the relationship between the premises and the conclusion, and compare this relationship to other arguments that we also reject as intuitively unacceptable. The remarkable thing is that the same few patterns appear over and over again. These patterns are then classified and can be used for immediate appraisals of arguments.

As we shall see in the chapter 3, the particular pattern of the foregoing unacceptable argument is called a violation of the rule of the undistributed middle. This terminology means nothing to the reader at the moment, but it does indicate that memorizing a few rules and being able to identify the patterns will enable him to spot immediately those arguments that are unacceptable for reasons of form, that is, because of the relationship between premises and conclusion.

We shall call all unacceptable arguments that violate the rules of form *invalid*. Any argument that does not violate these rules will be called *valid*.

There is yet another sense in which an argument can be unacceptable. An argument may be formally valid, that is its form may be acceptable, but we might reject the truth or acceptability of the premises. Analogously, a sentence may be grammatically correct but still false. An argument may be formally correct or valid but still not contain true premises. When an argument is valid but at least one of its premises is false, the argument is said to be *unsound*. When an argument is both formally valid and its premises are all true, then the argument is said to be *sound*. The ideal argument is, of course, a sound argument.

Formal logic is concerned exclusively with validity and invalidity. Logic by itself, or formal logic, does not determine the truth of its premises. Informal logic, on the other hand, is concerned with the soundness of arguments.

It may seem like an obvious matter to determine the truth or falsity of premises, and therefore an issue for science or expertise rather than logic. But the matter is not quite so obvious. The premises offered in an argument might be true but not relevant to the conclusion. So relevant truth becomes an issue. Alternatively, the premises may have the appearance of being true but are not really true. Exposing or utilizing deceptive presentations becomes an issue. Finally, there is the issue of interpreting truths; this, too, calls for judgments that may be challenged. Although informal logic cannot codify and classify all of the ways in which arguments are unsound and at the same time provide us with a simple mechanism in the way that formal logic does, it is nevertheless true that there is a remarkable recurrence of patterns even here. We shall be studying some of those patterns in the remainder of this book.

SUMMARY

1. *Logic* is the study of arguments.

2. *Arguments* are composed of a *conclusion* and one or more premises. The *premises* are evidence for the conclusion.

3. Arguments may be evaluated as either valid or invalid. An argument is *valid* if it is not invalid. An argument is *invalid* if it violates the rules. The rules are determined by studying the patterns of arguments whose premises are true and whose conclusion is false.

4. Arguments may also be evaluated as sound or unsound. An argument is *sound* if it is formally valid and its premises are all true. An argument is *unsound* if it is formally valid but at least one of its premises is false. Informal logic is concerned with all of the ways in which an argument might be unsound.

Two

Identifying Arguments

ARGUMENTS

As we have seen in chapter 1, logic is concerned with the structure of arguments. Arguments are composed of premises and a conclusion, where the premises are said to support, prove, or provide evidence for the conclusion. Before one can study the structure of an argument and evaluate the evidence of the premises, one must be able to identify an argument and the parts that compose it.

DIFFICULTIES IN IDENTIFYING ARGUMENTS

Not everything that is written contains an argument. In fact, most writing does not contain arguments. Quite often authors are only interested in defining a term, comparing and contrasting two ideas, describing an experience or event, or simply amusing or shocking readers. The different forms that writing might take and the purposes such writing might serve are so numerous that it would be impossible to list all of them.

Not only are the forms of discourse numerous, but it is also frequently difficult to decide which one(s) is (are) actually present in a text. Authors rarely begin a work by announcing their purpose and describing their method. In some cases (e.g., satire) such a beginning would destroy the author's whole effect. Moreover, authors—with the possible exception of those who write books on logic—do not proclaim at every point that they are presenting an argument; they do not label each and every sentence they write as either a premise or a conclusion.

GRAMMAR, PUNCTUATION, AND READING COMPREHENSION

Since this is not a book on reading comprehension and grammar; detailed instructions on how to read cannot be given. On the other hand, it should be emphasized that arguments cannot be identified and understood if the reader is unfamiliar with the mechanics of grammar and punctuation. There are two items that deserve special mention: pronouns and punctuation.

Consider the following statement from Thomas Hobbes's *Leviathan*:

> Whensoever a man transferreth his right, or renounceth it; it is either in consideration of some right reciprocally transferred to himself, or for some other good he hopeth for thereby. For *it* is a voluntary act; and of the voluntary acts of every man, the object is some good to himself.

Let us begin by asking what does the underscored word "it" refer to? An understanding of the pronoun "it" is absolutely essential to an understanding of Hobbes's argument. The pronoun "it" refers to the whole phrase "whensoever a man transferreth his right, or renounceth it." How do we know this? To begin with, a pronoun refers to an antecedent, that is, to a word or phrase that comes before the pronoun. Next, a pronoun agrees with its antecedent in number, that is, if a pronoun is singular then the antecedent must be singular. The pronoun "it" is singular and must therefore refer to a singular antecedent.

In Hobbes's statement there are several singular antecedents. Usually, the immediately preceding noun with the same number is the antecedent. The immediately preceding singular noun is "good." But a good is not an act. There are two other clues: context and structure. Structurally, there is another "it" that has as its antecedent the singular phrase "whensoever . . . renounceth it." Moreover, from the context the only act mentioned was the transferring and renouncing of a right. Consequently, it is plausible to assume that "it" refers to the transferring and renouncing of a right.

Let us consider another element of the same statement. "For it is a voluntary; and of the voluntary acts of every man, the object is some good to himself." A semicolon (;) appears in the middle of the sentence. The function of a semicolon is to connect grammatical units of equal rank. That is, we use a semicolon to connect two main clauses not joined by "and," "for," or some similar conjunctive term, and between two units containing commas. In our example, we have two equal units, each of which could be a separate sentence: (1) "it is a voluntary act" and (2) "of the voluntary acts of every man, the object is some good to himself." Hobbes, the author, places both clauses in the same sentence even though they could be separated. This means that he wants to emphasize their relatedness. That is, both clauses are to be treated together. The reason for a semicolon before the "and" instead of a comma is that the second clause already contains a comma.

What does all of this mean? As we shall see below in our discussion of rules for identifying premises, the word "for" signifies that whatever follows in the same grammatical unit is a premise. In our example, two things follow the word "for" in the same grammatical unit. Thus, we may conclude that Hobbes's statement has at least two premises: (1) "it is a voluntary act" (premise one); (2) "of the voluntary acts of every man, the object is some good to himself" (premise two). The semicolon or the comma before a coordinating conjunction (e.g., "and") signifies a unity. In this way, we were able to identify how many premises followed the word "for."

From our discussion of the role of pronouns, we know that the pronoun "it" refers to "the renouncing or the transferring of a right." If we substitute this information into the example, we obtain the following:

Premise one: Transferring or renouncing a right is a voluntary act.

Premise two: The object of every man's voluntary act is some good to himself. (Notice that we have modified the second premise into a more convenient form without changing its meaning.)

Even without knowing any logic, the reader can see that a conclusion suggests itself simply from reading the two premises. What conclusion? We can conclude that transferring or renouncing a right is an action performed with the intention of gaining some good for the agent. When we look at the original statement by Hobbes, we find that this is exactly what he says in the very first sentence.

Conclusion: "Whensoever a man transferreth his right, or renouceth it; it is either in consideration of some right reciprocally transferred to himself, or for some other good he hopeth for thereby."

RULES FOR IDENTIFYING
PREMISES AND CONCLUSIONS

Rule one: We do *not* identify premises and conclusions by content.

Rule two: We do *not* identify premises and conclusions by position or location within a paragraph. For stylistic or other reasons, the premises and the conclusions can appear anywhere.

Rule three: The appearance of the following word or words at the beginning of a sentence or clause signifies that the sentence or clause is a *conclusion: therefore, thus, so, hence, consequently, accordingly, it follows that, as a result, I conclude,* and synonymous terms.

In the following arguments, the conclusion is identified as the clause following the underscored words.

> Argument I: All men are mortal. Socrates is a man. *Therefore,* Socrates is mortal.

> Argument II: It rained yesterday, *so* I feel confident that the reservoir is full.

> Argument III: *Thus,* after having thought well on this matter, and after examining all things with care, I must finally *conclude* and maintain that this proposition: I am, I exist, is necessarily true every time that I pronounce it or conceive it in my mind. (Descartes)

Rule four: The appearance of the following word or words at the beginning of a sentence or clause signifies that the sentence or clause is a *premise: since, for, because, whereas, as, inasmuch as, seeing that,* and synonymous terms.

In the following argument, the premises are identified as the clause or clauses following the underscored words.

> Argument: *Since* Mr. Rivera is an alien, and *because* no aliens can vote in U.S. elections, we must conclude that Mr. Rivera cannot vote in the next election.

There is another common pattern found in arguments. Often we find two sentences or clauses flanking the words "for" or "because." When this pattern appears (as in the case of the previous argument from Hobbes, it means that what precedes "for" or "because" is a conclusion, and what follows "for" or "because" is one or more premises.

"………. for ………."
  (C)   (P)

"……………. because ……………."
(conclusion)   (premise)

Rule five: Supply implicit or missing premises and conclusions.
Many times an argument is so clear from its context that the
author provides only part of it. In these cases it is up to the
reader to supply the missing or assumed premises or even the
conclusion. This kind of argument is referred to as an
enthymeme.

Consider the following example. "Mr. Wong is an illegal
alien, so he is not permitted to vote." We can identify the part of
the sentence following "so" as the conclusion. The first part is a
premise. However, there is another obvious premise that is not
stated, namely, that "illegal aliens are not permitted to vote." The
complete argument now looks like this:

> Premise: Illegal aliens are not permitted to vote. (supplied
> by the reader)
> Premise: Mr. Wong is an illegal alien.
> _____
> Conclusion: Mr. Wong is not permitted to vote.

Rule six: Any proposition may be both a premise and a conclusion when there is more than one argument in the same
passage. A set of interlocking arguments is called a *sorites*
(sor-ī-tēz). The conclusion to one argument may be the
premise to the second argument.

The standard form for the presentation of a sorites is as
follows:

> Argument I:
> Premise (1): _____
> Premise (2): _____
> Conclusion₁: _____
>
> Argument II:
> Premise (1): (usually the conclusion of Argument I)
> Premise (2): _____
> Conclusion₂: _____

Sample Problem One

Consider the following sorites from Aristotle's *Politics*:

> Every state is a community of some kind, and every com-
> munity is established with a view to some good; *for* mankind
> always act in order to obtain that which they think good.
> But, if all communities aim at some good, the state or politi-
> cal community, *which* is the highest of all, and *which* em-
> braces all the rest, aims at good in a greater degree than any
> other, and at the highest good.

A careful reading of the passage reveals that Aristotle is talking
about the state. In fact, the passage looks as if it is a long description, or definition, of the state. An examination of the pronouns
and punctuation reveals the following. In the first sentence, a
semicolon appears and breaks up the sentence before the word
"for," a key clue. The second sentence begins with a repetition of
the same point made in the first sentence but adds something
extra. The additions include two clauses beginning with relative
pronouns. These clauses are descriptions of some of the character-
istics of the state. The second sentence then ends by ascribing a
new property to the state, a characteristic we did not find in the
first sentence.

When we look for clues to help identify premises and conclusions, we find one important clue, the word "for." We know that
what precedes "for" is a conclusion and what follows is a premise.
Therefore, the clause "every state is a community of some kind,
and every community is established with a view to some good" is
a conclusion. Moreover, we know now that the clause "mankind
always act in order to obtain that which they think good" is a
premise.

There is something else worth noticing about the first sentence. Given what it says, we may add to it a missing or implicit
premise, namely, that a community is the product of human
activity. We then obtain the following argument:

Argument I:

Premise (1): Mankind always act in order to obtain that which they think good. (the clue here is the word "for")

Premise (2): A community is the product of human activity. (implicit premise)

Conclusion: Every community is established with a view to some good. (the clue here is that this clause precedes the word "for")

We may now return to the main line of thought. There is still one unused part of the first sentence, namely, "every state is a community of some kind." Since this also precedes the word "for," we know that it depends upon the premise established by "for." But we already have a conclusion indicated by what precedes "for." Clearly what we have is yet another argument dependent upon what was established by the word "for."

Argument II:

Premise (1): Every community is established with a view to some good. (Conclusion$_1$)

Premise (2): Every state is a community of some kind.

Conclusion$_2$: Every state is established with a view to some good.

We may now complete the argument by adding the new or additional information present in the remainder of the passage.

Argument III:

Premise (1): Every state is established with a view to some good. (Conclusion$_2$)

Premise (2): The state is a political community which is the highest of all communities and which embraces all the rest.

Conclusion$_3$: The state aims at good in a greater degree than any other community, and at the highest good.

Sample Problem Two

The following passage is taken from the famous eighteenth-century British philosopher Bishop Berkeley in his work *A Treatise Concerning the Principles of Human Knowledge.*

> It is indeed an opinion strangely prevailing amongst men, that houses, mountains, rivers and in a word all sensible objects, have an existence, natural or real, distinct from their being perceived by the understanding. But, with how great an assurance and acquiescence soever this *Principle* may be entertained in the world, yet whoever shall find in his heart to call it in question may, if I mistake not, perceive it to involve a manifest contradiction. *For,* what are the aforementioned objects but the things we perceive by sense? and what do we perceive besides our own ideas or sensations? and is it not plainly repugnant that any of these, or any combination of them should exist unperceived?

Sentence one, "It is indeed . . . understanding," simply says (when transposed into contemporary English) that some people have the strange belief that sensible objects exist independently of perception. So far we do not know if this is a premise or a conclusion.

Sentence two, "But . . . to involve a manifest contradiction," says that the belief mentioned in sentence one is contradictory or false. Instead of having two sentences, we could reduce what Berkeley says to one sentence, namely, "The belief that houses, mountains, rivers . . . all sensible objects have an existence distinct from being perceived is a contradiction."

The third and final sentence begins with the word "for." Immediately, we know that our previously reconstructed sentence is a conclusion and that what follows the word "for" is a premise or set of premises. Sentence three also has some noteworthy punctuation. It contains three rhetorical questions, that is, questions that do not require an answer since they are really meant to be assertions with which the author expects you to agree. The word "for" covers all three rhetorical questions (disguised assertions) as seen by the fact that they are part of the same sentence, since none of them begins with a capital letter.

We are now ready to present the argument. Since there are three premises, we could present the argument as having three premises and one conclusion. However, as soon as we list the first two premises an implicit conclusion is suggested. So there must be at least two arguments.

Argument I:

Premise (1): Houses, mountains, rivers, etc., are things we perceive by sense. ("aforementioned objects" refers to houses, mountains, rivers, etc.)

Premise (2): Whatever we perceive are our own ideas or sensations.

Conclusion₁: Houses, mountains, rivers, etc., are our own ideas or sensations. (implicit conclusion)

Argument II:

Premise (1): Houses, mountains, rivers, etc., are our own ideas or sensations. (Conclusion₁)

Premise (2): None of our ideas or sensations, or any combination of them, can exist unperceived. ("any of these" refers to ideas or sensations)

Conclusion₂: The belief that houses, mountains, rivers, etc., have an existence distinct from their being perceived is a contradiction.

Three

Formal Analysis of Arguments

The purpose of this chapter is twofold: to summarize that part of traditional Aristotelian logic which is useful in analyzing arguments, and to indicate how informal logic may be viewed as a highly developed subdivision of traditional logic.

THE IDEAL OF LOGIC

Since the time of the classical Greeks, the ideal of logic has been the structure of an argument patterned after geometry. The mathematical ideal served Plato as a model for all good explanations. A good explanation is like a geometric proof, i.e., a deduction from first principles such that if the first principles (which serve as premises) are true, then the conclusion must be true. Example:

> All triangles are closed three-sided figures.
> That object is a triangle.
>
> Therefore, that object is a closed three-sided figure.

Even Aristotle accepted this as the model of a good explanation. However, whereas Plato thought that the very first principles or originating premises were known to be true through some sort of rational intuition, Aristotle insisted that the very first principles or originating premises were abstracted from experience. Example:

> All men are mortal.
> Socrates is a man.
>
> Therefore, Socrates is mortal.

For Aristotle, the truth of the major premise, "All men are mortal," is known from experience. The movement from individual experiences or facts like "Sophocles is mortal" and "Creon is mortal" to the general truth "All men are mortal" is called *induction,* but the movement from the general truth "All men are mortal" to "Socrates is mortal" is called *deduction.*

The ideal of logic has always been a deductive argument that begins with some general truth of the form "All *x*s are *y*s." The Western mind has subsequently constructed and reconstructed all arguments as deductuve arguments, which begin with some alleged general truth or even a general norm. Example:

> We should never negotiate with blackmailers.
> Terrorists are blackmailers.
> _____
> Therefore, we should never negotiate with terrorists.

Questions of form aside, the controversial issues are whether (a) we have identified the right generalization (whether it is a general definition, fact, norm, or whatever), and (b) the case we are dealing with at present is an example of that generalization. While formal logic is focused on the form or structure of an argument, informal logic is concerned with disputes about (a) and (b). Before we can launch into informal logic though, we must keep in mind the structural elements. Once we know the correct form (rules of validity) we can always reconstruct an argument, our own or someone else's, in order to make it valid. In the reconstruction process we articulate the previously unexpressed premises needed to make an argument formally valid. At the same time we thereby isolate the premises that might be controversial and serve as the subject matter of informal logic. Knowing which of our premises are controversial is important so that we may provide them with extra support or clarification, disguise them in the hope of eluding attack, or perhaps realize that they are indefensible and should be surrendered. Knowing which premises of our enemy's position are most controversial is important so that we can focus our counterattack in the most vulnerable spot.

SYLLOGISMS

In this chapter and throughout the book we have been implicitly following the practice for using, for the most part, arguments that have consisted of two premises. Such arguments having two premises are known as syllogisms. The reason they are used so often is more than a matter of convenience and tradition. All arguments can be reconstructed as syllogisms, that is, as having two premises and a conclusion. In addition, such reconstructed arguments are easier to follow. Most important, as we shall see below, informal logic can be usefully viewed as an exercise in syllogistic reasoning involving some very questionable suppressed premises.

Although there are several different kinds of syllogisms, we shall be concerned here with categorical syllogisms. A categorical syllogism is a syllogism in which all of the statements, both premises and the conclusion, are categorical statements. A statement is categorical if it is of the subject-predicate form. That is, it is a statement with four distinguishable parts: a quantifier, a subject, a copula, and a predicate. The following four statements are categorical:

quantifier	subject	copula	predicate	code
1. All	Xs	are	Ys	A
2. No	Xs	are	Ys	E
3. Some	Xs	are	Ys	I
4. Some	Xs	are not	Ys	O

I have used the same subject matter for the sake of convenience. We are not concerned here with the truth or falsity of these statements but only their form.

Categorical statements may also be classified as either affirmative or negative. Statements one and three above are *affirmative* in that they affirm something (namely the predicate) of the subject. Statements two and four are *negative* in that they deny something of the subject (namely the predicate). When we talk about the statements being affirmative or negative we are speaking of the *quality* of the statement.

In addition to a quality, statements have quantity. The quantity of a statement refers to the relationship between the quantifier and the subject term. There are three kinds of quantity: universal, particular, and singular. A statement is *universal* when the subject term refers to the entire class of objects that it names. Thus statements one and two above are universal in that they both refer to the entire class of Xs. A statement is *particular* when the subject term does not refer to the entire class of objects it names; rather it refers only to *some* part of that class. Thus statements three and four above are particular in that they both refer to some part of the class of Xs.

A statement is *singular* when the subject term is a proper name referring to a single individual. Our chart above does not include any examples of singular statements. An example would be the following: "Aristotle was a great logician." Another example is "Bob Dylan is not a logician." By convention, all singular statements are treated as universal statements on the grounds that they refer to the whole of the subject (all of Aristotle, all of Bob Dylan). In addition, the example about Aristotle is affirmative and the example about Bob Dylan is negative. Using the code from the chart above, the statement about Aristotle is an A statement, like "All Xs are Ys," and the statement about Bob Dylan is an E statement, like "No Xs are Ys."

Again, using the code letters A, E, I, and O, we summarize our discussion so far in the following:

A: Universal affirmative   I: Particular Affirmative
E: Universal negative   O: Particular negative

The concept of quantity refers primarily to the relationship of subject term and quantifier. Quantity overlaps with another concept, distribution, which refers to the predicate term as well as to the subject term. A term (either subject or predicate) is *distributed* if it refers to the whole class it names. A term is *undistributed* if it refers not to the whole class it names, but to only part of the class. As is obvious from our discussion of quantity, the subject of an A statement (all Xs) and the subject of an E statement (no Xs) are both distributed. Moreover, the subject of an I statement (some Xs) and an O statement (some Xs) are both undistributed. Now let us examine the predicates.

The predicate of an A statement ("All Xs are Ys") is undistributed since we are not referring to all Ys. The predicate of an E statement ("No Xs are Ys") is distributed since we are saying that nowhere in the entire class of Ys will we find an X. The predicate of an I statement ("Some Xs are Ys") is undistributed since, again, we are not referring to all Ys. The predicate of an O statement ("Some Xs are not Ys") is distributed since we can only say that some Xs are excluded from the class of Ys if we have excluded them from the entire class of Ys. The discussion of distribution now looks like this:

Statement	Subject	Predicate
A	distributed	undistributed
E	distributed	distributed
I	undistributed	undistributed
O	undistributed	distributed

There is one other set of relationships among statements that should be noted. A *contradiction* exists between two statements if they both cannot be true or both cannot be false at the same time. A and O are contradictories: If "All Xs are Ys" is true, then "Some Xs are not Ys" must be false, and vice versa. Two statements are said to be contraries if it is possible for both to be false but not possible for both to be true at the same time. A and E are contraries since it is possible for "All Xs are Ys" and "No Xs are Ys" both to be false if it is the case that only some Xs are Ys. At the same time, if "All Xs are Ys" is true, then "No Xs are Ys" cannot be true.

One could embarrass an opponent by attacking the contrary of an argument rather than its contradictory. Take the following example: You wish to argue the A statement that "All Communists are bad" and your opponent wishes to argue that "Some Communists are not bad," which is an O statement. In attacking him you pretend that his position is an E and not an O and attack with ease the E proposition "No Communists are bad." While both of you cannot be right—that is, one of you must be wrong either way—the attack on E allows for both of you to be wrong. This is a safety valve in case you find yourself trapped.

The traditional square of opposition brings out the foregoing relationships.

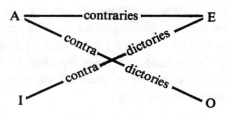

Now that we have examined and defined the properties of categorical statements, it is time to turn our attention to categorical syllogisms. Each statement has two terms, a subject term and a predicate term. Since a syllogism has two premises and a conclusion (a total of three statements), there is a grand total of six terms. However, in a syllogism each of those terms appears twice. Thus a categorical syllogism has three terms each of which appears twice. Example:

> All carp are fish.
> All fish are found in water.
> Therefore, all carp are found in water.

As you can see, "fish" appears twice, "carp" appears twice, and "found in water" appears twice.

We may next distinguish among the major, minor, and middle terms. The *major term* is that term which appears as the predicate of the conclusion. In our example above, "found in water" is the major term. The premise that contains the other appearance of the major term is called the major premise, and in our example "All fish are found in water" is the major premise. The *minor term* is that term which appears as the subject of the conclusion. In our example above, "carp" is the minor term. The premise that contains the other appearance of the minor term is called the minor premise, and in our example "All carp are fish" is the minor premise. Thus every categorical syllogism consists of a major premise, a minor premise, and a conclusion. The *middle term* is the term that appears in both premises. In our example above, "fish" is the middle term.

RULES FOR VALID SYLLOGISMS

We are now ready to test syllogisms. We distinguish between valid and invalid syllogisms. In a *valid* categorical syllogism, if both premises are true then the conclusion must be true. Logicians have been able to work out a few rules such that any syllogism that violates these rules is invalid, and any syllogism that does not violate the rules is automatically valid. Thus we might speak of the rules for invalidating the syllogism.

First, an example of a valid syllogism that is in essence the basic format of all valid syllogistic arguments:

> All carp are fish.
> All fish are animals.
>
> All carp are animals.

Another version of this same essential form is:

> All men are mortal.
> Socrates is a man.
>
> Socrates is mortal.

A final version:

> All children like candy.
> Some members of my family are children.
>
> Some members of my household like candy.

There are three rules, the violation of any of which automatically shows the categorical syllogism to be invalid.

First Rule: The middle term must be distributed at least

once. This rule is the only rule that is seriously and frequently violated in everyday reasoning. For example:

All Communists are in favor of reform.
All liberals are in favor of reform.

All liberals are Communists.

In the above argument, the middle term is "in favor of reform." Both premises, in which the middle term occurs, are A statements and the middle term is the predicate in both premises. We know from our chart above on distrubution that the predicate of an A statement is never distributed. Therefore, the middle term is not distributed at least once and the argument is invalid. The fallacy of *guilt by association* is a form of this kind of invalidity.

Second Rule: A term that is distributed in the conclusion must be distributed in one of the premises. For example:

All radicals are in favor of reform.
No conservatives are radicals.

No conservatives are in favor of reform.

In the above statement, we have an E statement for the conclusion "No conservatives are in favor of reform." Thus both the subject and the predicate are distributed. However, in the major premise "All radicals are in favor of reform," which is an A statement, the predicate "in favor of reform" cannot be distributed. Thus there is a term "in favor of reform" that is distributed in the conclusion but not in one of the premises and the argument is invalid.

Knowing this rule is especially important when your opponent employs an argument with a suppressed premise. Suppose your opponent uses the following argument: "Since no conservatives are radicals they cannot be in favor of reform." Your reply is twofold. First, you reconstruct your opponent's argument in order to make it valid; supply the missing premise that would make it valid ("All those in favor of reform are radicals"), and ask him if this is what he means. If he says yes, then obviously he is making a false statement and he is embarrassed in front of the audience. Presumably everyone knows that radicals are not the only people in favor of reform. Second, you reconstruct your opponent's argument to make it invalid and supply the missing premise that would make it invalid ("All radicals are in favor of reform") and then expose the argument as invalid and your opponent as a logical ignoramus.

Third Rule: The number of negative premises must be the same as the number of negative conclusions. This rule sounds odd but just think of the possibilities. Since there is one conclusion *(a)* if the conclusion is negative then there must be one, and only one, negative premise. As soon as there are two negative premises the argument is automatically invalid. *(b)* If the conclusion is affirmative there can be no negative premises. If there is a negative premise there must be a negative conclusion.

For example: Suppose your opponent argues that "Country X is not a capitalist country, therefore Country X respects the working man." There is no possible way of making this a valid argument.

All (or No) countries that respect the working man are capitalist countries.

Country X is not a capitalist country.
_____

∴ Country X is a country that respects the working man.

Either way the above argument is invalid. The only way to get to the affirmative conclusion desired is to present the affirmative argument:

All noncapitalist countries are countries that respect the working man.

Country X is a noncapitalist country.
_____

∴ Country X is a country that respects the working man.

However, by making the argument valid we expose its Achilles heel or its most questionable point. Why should we accept the statement that "All noncapitalist countries are countries that respect the working man'"? Not only is this sentence not intuitively obvious, it is downright false. Once again, knowing the rules helps us to expose the implicit generalizations of your opponent's case.

The point behind these three rules can be put more intuitively. The first rule about the undistributed middle tells us that things which are alike in one respect may not be alike in other or all other respects. The second rule about distribution tells us that the strength of the conclusion cannot exceed the strength of the premises. The conclusion cannot be more general (have a greater distribution) or go beyond what is implicit in the premises. The third rule shows that we cannot reach a positive conclusion from purely negative premises. To show that a thing lacks one quality does not by itself prove that it has another. To reach a positive or affirmative conclusion we must at some point introduce one or more affirmative premises. However, negative conclusions can be arrived at by a combination of both positive and negative information. Even a negative conclusion requires some positive backing.

For those readers who are delving more deeply into syllogistic logic, please note that these rules do not cover cases involving the so-called existential fallacy.

SOUNDNESS AND INFORMAL LOGIC

We have defined a valid argument as one that does not violate the rules so that *if* its premises are true *then* its conclusion must be true. However, this does not mean that a valid argument automatically has true premises. *Arguments can be valid and still have false premises.*

However, when an argument is valid (i.e., it does not violate the rules) and its premises are known to be true, then we say it is a *sound* argument.

It is my contention that one rarely finds invalid arguments in daily life. On the other and, one finds an incredible number of unsound arguments. This is precisely why knowing about the syllogism is useful. By reconstructing your opponent's arguments to make them valid, and thereby bringing out the implicit premise (usually the major premise), you can put your finger on some generalization that might be weak enough to be attacked. We have seen this in the second and third rules above. When you attack that premise as untrue you are accusing your opponent of having an unsound argument.

Further, most, if not all, of the traditional *fallacies of informal logic* may be viewed as *valid* arguments *but* with an unacceptable major premise, and therefore as *unsound arguments*. For example, the fallacy of composition is the fallacy of believing that what is true of all the parts is true of the whole:

> All that is true of the parts *is* true of the whole.
> All of the parts of a locomotive are light.
>
> Therefore, a (whole) locomotive is light.

Since the argument is valid but the conclusion is false (or unacceptable), one of the premises must be false (or unacceptable).

The fallacious use of the *ad populum* is an appeal to the major premise that what most people like is good. Consider the following argument:

> Whatever book most people like is great literature.
> Most people like *Love Story*.
>
> Therefore, *Love Story* is great literature.

The second premise is true if one judges by best seller lists. The conclusion is considered false by many literary experts. At the same time, the argument s logically valid. The only way of challenging the conclusion is to argue that the major premise ("Whatever book most people like is great literature") is false, and therefore that the argument is unsound.

The *ad baculum,* or the appeal to force, can also be viewed as an instance of an unsound argument. Consider the following argument:

Whenever I threaten you is a time when you must
do as I say.
Now is a time I threaten to raise your taxes if you
do not vote for Smith.

Now is a time that you must do as I say (vote for Smith).

The argument is valid but unsound if you reject as false the premise that you must do as I say whenever I threaten you.

I shall leave to the reader the task of working out examples of other well-known fallacies. Knowing syllogistic logic thus helps to analyze the weak points in your opponent's arguments.

Four

Presenting Your Case

In presenting your case to other people, there are several general considerations that must be kept in mind. First, you must have a clear idea of just what your case, issue, or point of view is. Second, you must be aware of the relation of your position on this case or issue to your position on other issues. The reason for this is obvious. You do not want to present your case on one issue in such a way that it might cause conflicts or future embarrassments when you present your position on another issue. Third, you should have some clear idea of the audience to whom you are presenting your case. Are they people who already share your opinion, are they undecided, or are they likely to be unreceptive or openly hostile? No doubt your audience may consist of any combination of the foregoing possibilities. Different audiences will require different approaches. Fourth, you must understand the medium you are using to convey your case. Are you speaking directly to the people, or are you writing an article for a newspaper, magazine, scholarly journal or the like? Are you preparing an advertisement that will be visually presented for a few moments; an audio commercial that lasts thirty seconds; a mimeographed sheet that will be read in one minute and discarded; a placard to be waved about, . . .? Finally, you must constantly keep in the forefront of your mind the purpose for which you are presenting your case. If you are a rational teacher trying to present an objective case you will do one thing (like considering the shortcomings of your position), and if you are trying to get people to buy a product you will do something else (like pretending that there are no weaknesses in your product).

The last point is worth dwelling upon. If you know what you want to achieve (your purpose), and if you know the people with whom you want to achieve your end (your audience), and the means available to you (medium), then you will be better able to achieve your end. No doubt there are all kinds of clever and brilliant things you might do, but it is equally clear that some of these clever and brilliant things may be irrelevant, in which case they may detract attention from your main purpose or even be counterproductive. If you remember that the important thing is winning, then you are not likely to go off in all directions at once. Analogously, there is no reason for leading a dazzling and disastrous cavalry charge (however immortal this may make you in the hearts of poets) when a simple artillery barrage will do the job.

In the discussion to follow, I will assume that the audience is either present, in which case the presentation is oral, or that the audience is being communicated with through some journalistic medium. Where more specialized audiences are involved, I shall note the special techniques required. Otherwise it is to be assumed that the audience is listening to your speech or reading it.

The presentation of your case should be given in three main parts: arousing sympathy for your cause; presenting facts, or what will be taken as facts, to substantiate your case; and driving home the conclusion. The first three parts of this chapter will consider each of these in greater detail. The fourth will consider some nonverbal techniques to be used in presenting your case.

Part of the reason for the complexity of arguments is that audiences are not monolithic. That is, in presenting a case we have to appeal to people whose interests are not uniform. There are at least six different types of audiences from the point of view of audience interest.

1. The audience may consist of people who agree with your end or ultimate goal.

2. The audience may consist of people who agree both with your end or ultimate goal and with the means you are suggesting for reaching it.

3. The audience may consist of people who agree with your end but only as a means to some other end that they do not share with you. What is an end for you, therefore, may be a means for them.

4. The audience may consist of people who agree with your means but seek thereby to achieve different ends. In other words, what you have in common is means but not ends.

5. There are of course combinations of the above where some of the audience agree on the end and some agree only on your end as a means to their somewhat different goals. This is a combination of (1) and (2) above.

6. There are complex audiences wherein an end for you is a means to them, but the additional end they foresee is an acceptable end for you as well. This is a combination of (3) and (4). Here you must argue for something as both a means and an ultimate end at the same time.

GAINING A SYMPATHETIC AUDIENCE

The notion that one can engage in argumentation by simply launching into the presentation of information is a foolish one. No discussion, and certainly no argument, can exist in a vacuum. Everyone, including the speaker and the audience, has a frame of reference in terms of which he speaks and to which he implicitly or explicitly appeals. It is essential that you keep this frame of reference in mind when presenting your case. If you want to prepare the audience for the presentation of your point of view and to gain a sympathetic hearing as well, then appeal to the common frame of reference that you share with the audience.

Appeal to Pity

To appeal to pity is to appeal to the emotions of your audience, emotions that you expect to be favorably directed to your cause.

The most effective use of the appeal to pity does *not* involve the use of highly emotive and inflammatory language; rather it relies upon the bare presentation of simple and unchallengeable facts. It is important that this appeal not be overdone so that members of the audience are not unnecessarily antagonized. This is especially true when the audience is not well known to you or when they are still undecided about the issue raised.

Appeals to pity are found most frequently in courts of law where attorneys attempt to gain a sympathetic hearing for their clients. An example is to be found in the case of a young man who is on trial for burning down the house of his parents while they were sleeping and who has thus been charged with homicide. His attorney pleads for mercy on the grounds that the young man is now an orphan!

The most famous, and in a way clever and ironic, use of the appeal to pity is the one directed by Socrates to the jury trying him on the charges of impiety and corrupting the youth of Athens. The famous trial is described in Plato's dialogue titled the *Apology*.

> Perhaps there may be some one who is offended at me, when he calls to mind how he himself, on a similar or even a less serious occasion, prayed and entreated the judges with many tears, and how he produced his children in court, which was a moving spectacle, together with a host of relations and friends; whereas I, who am probably in danger of my life, will do none of these things. The contrast may occur to his mind, and he may be set against me, and vote in anger because he is displeased at me on this account. Now if there be such a person among you—mind, I do not say that there is—to him I may fairly reply: My friend, I am a man, and like other men, a creature of flesh and blood, and not "Of wood or stone," as Homer says; and I have a family, yes, and sons, O Athenians, three in number, one almost a man, and two others who are still young; and yet I will not bring any of them hither in order to petition you for an acquittal. And why not? Not from any self-assertion or want

of respect for you. . . . But, having regard to public opinion, I feel that such conduct would be discreditable to myself, and to you, and to the whole state. . . . And I say that these things ought not to be done by those of us who have a reputation; and if they are done, you ought not to permit them; you ought rather to show that you are far more disposed to condemn the man who gets up a doleful scene and makes the city ridiculous, than him who holds his peace.

Another well-known example of the appeal to pity is to be found in Marc Antony's speech in Shakespeare's play *Julius Caesar* (Act III, Scene 2);

Friends, Romans, countrymen, lend me your ears;
I come to bury Caesar, not to praise him.
The evil that men do lives after them;
The good is oft interred with their bones;
So let it be with Caesar. The noble Brutus
Hath told you Caesar was ambitious;
If it were so, it was a grievous fault,
And grievously hath Caesar answered it.
Here, under leave of Brutus and the rest,—
For Brutus is an honorable man;
So are they all, all honorable men,—
Come I to speak in Caesar's funeral.
He was my friend, faithful and just to me:
But Brutus says he was ambitious;
And Brutus is an honorable man.
He hath brought many captives to Rome,
Whose ransoms did the general coffers fill:
Did this in Caesar seem ambitious?
When that the poor have cried, Caesar hath wept;
Ambition should be made of sterner stuff:
Yet Brutus says he was ambitious;
And Brutus is an honorable man.
You all did see that on the Lupercal
I thrice presented him a kingly crown,

> Which he did thrice refuse: was this ambition?
> Yet Brutus says he was ambitious;
> And, sure, he is an honorable man.
> I speak not to disprove what Brutus spoke,
> But here I am to speak what I do know.
> You all did love him once, not without cause:
> What cause withholds you then to mourn for him?
> O judgment, thou art fled to brutish beasts,
> And men have lost their reason. Bear with me;
> My heart is in the coffin there with Caesar,
> And I must pause till it come back to me.

In a more contemporary vein, there are many examples of the presentation of an argument that begins with an appeal to pity. In presenting a case against the use of drugs or in favoring the imposition of a policy to curb drug addiction, we might begin by describing the life and death of a twelve-year-old boy who became a heroin addict. In arguing for pacificism, we might describe the horrors of war as in a description of the aftermath of the dropping of an atomic bomb on Hiroshima. The critics of the Vietnam War effectively employed the reading of lists of war dead as an appeal to pity. On the other hand, those who favor the policy of a strong military posture and preparedness might present their case by beginning with a description of the bombing of Pearl Harbor or a description of the concentration camp at Auschwitz, pointing out how these were partly the result of political isolationism.

Appeal to Authority

To appeal to authority is to inform your audience that prominent people are in favor of the position you are urging. The appeal to authority, like the appeal to pity, is an attempt to establish a frame of reference for the rest of your case. There is nothing inherently wrong with this appeal; rather, it is essential to any discussion. No one can know everything nor can he be everywhere at once. We are all forced to take for granted that other people are sometimes experts in their fields and that they are reliable sources of information. If the people who are engaged in a discussion, argument, or dispute cannot agree on authorities, then the prospects of a successful resolution are very dim indeed. Moreover, if you can appeal to the right authorities, you are also guaranteeing a more sympathetic hearing for your case.

There are at least eight qualifications that should be kept in mind when citing authorities. First, you should be sure that the authority you cite is not considered a liar by members of your audience. A man convicted of perjury is hardly a credible witness. A political leader who has once misled people loses his credibility in the eyes of the public. Adlai Stevenson suffered this fate in the United Nations because he, at one critical moment, denied that the United States had supported the invasion of Cuba during the Bay of Pigs episode.

Second, you must present authorities who are considered disinterested by the audience, that is, authorities who do not have a vested interest in the case you are discussing. The reason for this should be obvious. A man with a vested interest is tempted, either consciously or unconsciously, to construe things in his own favor. Naturally, this makes him an unreliable authority. In certain technical fields it is next to impossible to misconstrue the facts. Thus, in the case of handwriting analysis, ballistics, or chemical analysis, it is difficult to conceive of an interested authority. Anyway, it is always possible to find a disinterested one if you are sure that the facts will be on your side.

On the other hand, there are certain fields where finding a disinterested authority is next to impossible. I am thinking in particular about politics. Putting aside for the moment the question of whether there is even such a thing as an authority on political matters, there is the ever present problem of separating a disinterested analysis of a political situation from the interests, wants, needs, or hopes of the person doing the analysis. In an area such as this the closest thing to an authority would be someone with a distinguished record of predictions, even where those predictions ran contrary to the *known* interests of the predictor.

Examples of people whose possible interests might disqualify them as authorities worthy of being invoked follow. A stockbroker whose profits come from the volume of securities sold is not to be considered a disinterested authority on what to expect from the stock market. Such an interest can only be offset if the broker can substantiate the fact that he has successfully predicted in the past and that he has advised people against investing at certain times. In such a way he is establishing his integrity. In discussing appropriations for the military budget, it must be kept in mind that prominent military men have a vested interest in getting the largest appropriation possible. At the same time, members of the academic and research communities who have traditionally argued against large or increased military expenditures stand to gain themselves from a smaller military expenditure since there would be more funds available for the expansion of college and research facilities. Hence, they, too, might have a vested interest in such a controversy.

Third, the audience should consider the authority to be conscientious about the area in which he claims expertise. A man who is not careful about details will soon cease to be considered an authority. Moreover, an expert who relies upon the assistance of a large staff must be sure about the diligence of his staff. A cabinet officer who relies upon a huge bureaucracy can easily be tempted into accepting a report and then presenting it to the public without careful scrutiny. Most of us have noticed how painstakingly some scientists will make claims or to what lengths they will go in qualifying the implications of their research. Usually, it is the headline-hunting journalist who makes excessive claims.

Fourth, when an authority is invoked it is best to make sure that the authority is well known. Quoting authorities who are not known to be authorities in their fields, at least not known by your audience, is ineffective. For example, when discussing child rearing, it might be more impressive to refer to Gesell or Spock than to Dr. John Smith. "Well known" in this case is always to be determined by reference to your specific audience. Although a person is generally well known, he or she may not be well known in a particular area or to a particular audience. Conversely, when addressing a specific audience it might be better to quote the local expert than the internationally famous one.

Fifth, the authority used must be an expert in the relevant field. Dr. Spock may be a well-known expert in the field of child care, but can one honestly say that he is an expert in international relations in particular and politics in general? When discussing physics, it would seem natural to use physicists as authorities; when discussing the possibilities of using the sea to grow food, the relevant authorities would be marine biologists, and so on. To invoke an authority in one field as an expert in another, perhaps totally unrelated, field opens one to all kinds of damaging attacks. For example, a man once claimed to have invented a truly effective cigarette filter and offered to promote it under the sponsorship of Columbia University of New York City. Columbia may have an outstanding reputation in general as a university, but this in no way implies that everything associated with it is outstanding. Combined with a lack of conscientiousness on the part of some Columbia administrators, this carelessness led to all sorts of embarrassments. As far as I know, that filter is still unavailable.

The one important exception to the foregoing qualification of invoking authorities concerns the use of celebrities, prominent members of society either theatrical or "aristocratic." In a sense, these people are not necessarily experts in anything. However, their sheer prominence will attract attention to a cause or position in a way that no other appeal can match. On the assumption that one can provide relevant experts, there is no objection to supplementing those experts with celebrities who are not experts. A case in point concerns the campaign of the American Cancer Society to discourage cigarette smoking. There is no question that the American Cancer Society can provide authoritative evidence from medical authorities who are beyond reproach. But in addition to this authority, the society has employed well-known actors to dramatize the connection between cigarette smoking and cancer. This campaign has been highly effective. Think of actor Yul Bryner saying, "By the time you see this, I shall be dead. . . ."

Thus we see how qualification four (well known) and qualification five (relevant expert) may supplement each other. At the same time, we should not forget qualification three (being conscientious). One of the actors employed for the cigarette-danger campaign of the American Cancer Society was later arrested in London for the possession of marijuana.

Sixth, if possible, the authorities cited should be both current and historical. The more technical the issue, the more current should be your authority. Thus, in medical matters, possibly a question about the heart, Dr. Christian Barnard is more to be respected as an authority than Galen or Hippocrates. Statistical studies especially should be as fresh as possible. On the other hand, if one can find historical authority to supplement current authority, this has a way of making one's case even stronger. George Washington has a way of popping up in all kinds of arguments. He is sometimes paired with Senator Fulbright (the former as historical and the latter as a more contemporary authority) as an expert in arguing against entangling foreign alliances. I have also seen Washington invoked as a proponent, at least implicitly, of marijuana since he allegedly grew hemp in his fields and it was widely used during the eighteenth century to treat bronchitis. Here Washington might be paired with any current popular proponent of drug use.

Seventh, the authority cited should have an opinion that is representative of the general expertise in his field. The word "representative" is a tricky one to define, but it can perhaps be made clear through some examples. A great physicist may share many opinions with his colleagues, but he may also have some highly idiosyncratic opinions that are not shared or even are opposed by his colleagues, especially in controversial areas. A nuclear physicist who literally believes that life exists on other planets holds an unrepresentative opinion. In 1936, when Franklin D. Roosevelt was running for president of the United States, over two-thirds of the newspapers in the country were editorially opposed to his re-election. This percentage in no way represented the actual feeling of the community or even the people who actually worked for these newspapers. It was an opinion that simply reflected the position of those who owned the newspapers.

The eighth qualification is that the authorities should be as numerous, as diverse, and otherwise as different as possible. If you can find two authorities with otherwise conflicting opinions who nevertheless agree with your position on a specific issue, this tends to impress the audience with the fact that you are so right that almost everyone has to agree with you. For example, it would be foolish to quote the editorial opinion of one newspaper twice in order to support your case. Obviously once is enough. On the other hand, if you live in an area with two or more newspapers that usually have conflicting editorial frames of reference, but they for once agree on your position, then it is very impressive to quote from both. President Reagan has been very successful in quoting former presidents like Franklin D. Roosevelt and John F. Kennedy (democrats) in support of Republican policies.

Appeal to Tradition (Sacred Cows)

The appeal to tradition, also known as the *ad populum* appeal, is the appeal to an ideal, a theoretical or abstract principle to which all people—or at the very least the members of your audience—pay lip service. No doubt some people take these ideals more seriously than do other people, but everyone claims to respect them. This is an important principle of argumentation because it is one of those principles that establishes the frame of reference of the discussion. If you cannot find this common point then there cannot be any discussion at all. (You should keep in mind that this is definitely not an appeal to precedent, which will be discussed in the next subsection.)

An example of the appeal to tradition is Martin Luther King's invoking of the principle of nonviolence. Whie there are certainly those who would not under similar circumstances use nonviolence, or even those who do not subscribe to the principle in their heart of hearts, it is still the case that few would openly attack someone else's advocacy of nonviolence. The appeal to nonviolence is an appeal to a tradition that has deep moral, political, social, and religious roots, roots that spread beyond any one culture or historical period. To invoke nonviolence is to gain a tremendous sympathetic reaction on the part of audiences. We might also add that this principle can frequently disarm enemies as well.

Appeal to Precedent

To appeal to precedent is to appeal to cases or instances similar to the one being defended. It is not necessary that everyone agree with your precedent, as in the case of the appeal to tradition. Precedents must be real or actual as opposed to traditions, which are ideal. In fact, we frequently appeal to precedent when we cannot find a tradition to help us, but it must be recognized that this kind of appeal is a calculated risk in that it automatically antagonizes some part of the audience.

Violent revolution is a precedent in American life, as is obvious from our Revolutionary War and the Civil War, but it would be odd indeed to say that violent revolution is one of our ideals. When the radical black leader H. Rap Brown allegedly said that "violence is as American as apple pie," he was appealing to precedent and not to tradition.

The appeal to precedent is found most frequently in law courts where attorneys must search for cases previously decided in order to buttress their present case. If the courts, especially higher courts, have made decisions favorable to one "kind" of issue and if an attorney believes that his present case belongs to that "kind" or category, then he appeals to that decision or series of decisions as precedents. Needless to add, the other attorneys must find different precedents or show how the case does not fit the alleged "kind."

There is a story about a fig newton told by an ex-Supreme Court justice. Imagine one company suing another company, where both companies produce pastry and baked goods. The suit concerns patent rights. Company A claims that it owns a patent for a specific kind of cookie and that Company B has violated the patent by making a similar cookie. Company B claims that its product is different because it is not a cookie but a fig newton. When is a change a change? If the judge favors Company A he decides that the patent right has been violated, whereas if he supports Company B he might say that the product is really a fig newton and does not fall under the cookie patent. There are endless precedents, and finding the right one for your case involves (a) ingenuity in your research, and (b) knowing what appeals to your audience. Judges are not the only ones with definite tastes.

PRESENTING THE FACTS

Statistics

The purpose of this section is to show how the facts or the accepted truth should be used in presenting your case. The minor theme can be summed up in the statement that half a truth is sometimes better than no truth at all.

In an age such as ours, the most convincing kind of evidence is statistical evidence. What boy does not know the batting average, to three decimal places, of his favorite baseball player? How often have we heard one automobile praised at the expense of another because the former possesses a measurably greater miles per gallon ratio? The underlying assumption in so much of our use of numbers seems to be that a higher number automatically indicates something better. You cannot argue with numbers, except with other numbers.

Some general rules about using statistics follow. On the assumption that it is possible, always do the following when appealing to statistical evidence. First, make sure that the statistics come from a reliable source. Here all of the things we said about using authority will be relevant. The right source of statistical information can be epitomized in the expression "independent laboratory." Second, since statistical data are rarely uniform, they may be grouped or "interpreted" in different ways. Do not hesitate to use only that part of the statistical data which suits your case, especially if you do not expect to be challenged. For example, a national survey on how people feel about abortion may indicate that most or the majority are opposed to it. When the statistics are broken down by states, it may be that in your state the majority of the people favor it. Thus, if you wish to get a law passed favorable to abortions then quote the state statistics. If you wish to get a law passed against abortions then quote the national survey. In both cases you will be telling the truth.

This brings us to the third general rule, a rule we might dub "getting on the bandwagon." If you can show that most people, or the majority, support your position or opinion, then not only invoke that information as support or evidence that you are right, but also invite people or the audience, at least implicitly, to join the majority. No one likes to be left out in the cold.

An important variation of this general rule concerns the phrase "more people." How often have you heard the expression, "More people use Brand X than any other brand." What exactly does this mean? It can mean that 51 percent of all people use Brand X. It can also mean that only 12 percent of all people use Brand X. How is this possible? Suppose we have a situation in which there are sixteen competing brands of beer (or sixteen candidates for office). Isn't it possible that no one brand (or candidate) from among the sixteen has a majority and that the brand (or candidate) with the largest following has only 12 percent? It is not only possible but true to say that Brand X (or candidate X) has *more* followers than any other brand (or candidate). The phrase "more people . . ." may be invoked and used just as if it meant a majority.

A fourth general rule concerns the use of large numbers. Invariably, large numbers impress people much more than small numbers. When you add to this the fact that even in our society most people do not really comprehend the use of statistics, percentages, and fractions, it is usually more effective to quote the large number rather than the percentage. It sounds better to say that candidate Smith received six million votes than to say he received 52 percent of the votes. Almost half of the people voted against Smith but he sounds more formidable when you say that six million people are behind him.

We should also add that where large numbers are involved repeating them tends to have a mathematically cumulative effect. It is said that when the Soviet Union grants foreign aid to a country it grants at least three times more aid than it actually gives. How is this possible? For example, first it is announced in the press that the Soviet Union *will* grant one million dollars worth of aid. Second, when aid is actually granted it is once more announced that the Soviet Union *is* granting one million dollars worth of aid. Finally, after the aid has been granted it is announced that the Soviet Union *has* granted one million dollars in aid. Many people would have the impression that three million dollars in aid was involved.

Fifth, just as large numbers tend to impress, so small numbers tend to be overlooked. This means that you may openly discount a small number or minimize its importance. An example of this was supplied by Yugoslavia's Marshal Tito. In discussing political parties, Tito once observed that America has two political parties while Yugoslavia has one. It is an insignificant difference because it is only a difference of one!

It is now time to turn to some actual cases of the use of statistical data. No number is important in itself. It is only with respect to some other number or to some frame of reference that a particular number acquires its significance. Hence the important thing is not simply collecting data but selecting the frame of reference within which you plan to use the data.

In our example, let us imagine that a large and important corporation that deals in retail sales has just reported its financial record for the year. The relevant, and true, figures are as follows:

Earnings: (a) 1 percent of sales, *or*

(b) one percent on a dollar, *or*

  (c) 12 percent on investment, *or*
  (d) $5,000,000 profit, *or*
  (e) 40 percent increase in profits over 1939, *or*
  (f) 60 percent decrease in profits over last year.

All of these figures say exactly the same thing. A retail organization takes in a large gross but actual net receipts after expenses are very small. The first two figures, (a) and (b) reflect this fact. You may begin to wonder how in the world any corporation stays in business or would want to stay in a business for such a small profit margin. The answer is that daily sales bring in a large amount of cash that can then be invested at high interest rates for the remainder of the year. We are all familiar with the fact that the larger the amount of money you can invest, the larger the percentage of the return. The same one percent may, by the end of the year, return twelve percent. By the end of the year, the actual profit in dollars may be, as in (d), $5,000,000. How does this profit compare with past performance? It all depends, again, on the frame of reference. If we choose the 1939 level as base period, profits have increased substantially. If we choose last year's profits as the frame of reference, profits may have decreased even though the company is still earning a profit.

How would these statistics be used? The management would use them as follows: in refuting an argument for price controls, the management will refer to (a); in reporting to the stockholders, the management will refer to either (c), (d), or (e); in bargaining with the unions, the management will refer to (f). The union, of course, will insist upon (d) and (e) in demanding higher wages and benefits for the employees. Dissident stockholders may seize upon either (f) or challenge (c) as being too low and the result of poor investments, suggesting the need for a new board of directors.

Let us take another example. In the graph on the next page, we have reported the average income broken down by educational categories. As we go from left to right, income increases, and as we go from top to bottom educational attainment increases.

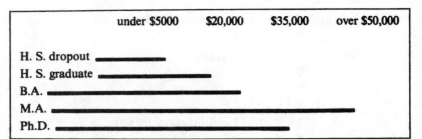

	under $5000	$20,000	$35,000	over $50,000
H. S. dropout	▬▬▬▬			
H. S. graduate	▬▬▬▬▬			
B.A.	▬▬▬▬▬▬▬▬			
M.A.	▬▬▬▬▬▬▬▬▬▬▬▬			
Ph.D.	▬▬▬▬▬▬▬			

In an effort to encourage students to gain as much education as possible, it has been frequently pointed out that income increases with education. The longer you stay in school, the more you are likely to earn during your lifetime. However, such an argument can be used only if we do not take into account the average earnings of Ph.Ds. If we drop out the last line, the Ph.D. line, the case will be more convincing. Conversely, if we retain only the last two lines, we would have a good case against continuing on for the Ph.D. degree.

Perhaps the most useful word in the statistical arsenal is the word *average.* The term "average" may mean one of three different things. First, it may mean the arithmetical *mean,* which is the total divided by the number of people or entities involved; second, it may mean the *median,* which is the halfway point between the number of people or entities involved; third, it may mean the *mode,* which is the point where you find more people or entities on the scale than at any other point.

Our example of differing uses of the term "average" is taken from the reading scores of a seventh grade class of students. A test is administered to determine the level at which the students are reading. To be on grade level is to be able to read what students at that grade are expected to read. For the seventh grade student in our example, to be on grade level is to be able to read what the seventh grade student is expected to read. To be reading below grade level is to be unable to reader' what the seventh grade student is expected to read. To be reading above grade level is to be able to read not only what the seventh grade student is expected to read but also much more difficult pieces.

Grade Level	Number of Students
12	4
11	4
10	3
9	2
8	1
7	1 (arithmetical mean)
6	0
5	1 (median, 15 above, 15 below)
4	2
3	12 (mode)

If we use "average" to mean arithmetical mean, then the teacher can legitimately claim that the class is reading at its grade level. If we use average in the sense of either median or mode, then critics of the teacher can legitimately say that the average member of the class is not reading at grade level. It is obvious, of course, that a serious problem exists in this class and it is equally obvious that any attempt to understand the problem in terms of averages would be misleading.

Suppose that I am contemplating a change of residence, and that I am looking for a more equable climate. I begin by reading advertisements and I find two areas with annual mean temperatures of 75 degrees. That sounds fine. However, one of these areas has a temperature range from 65 degrees to 85 degrees, whereas the other area has a temperature range from 35 degrees to 115 degrees. Obviously, they are not equally desirable.

The important principle that we have seen at work time and time again is that the same information may be presented in different ways. The trick is to choose the way most useful to your case. *Question:* Should one use total numbers or percentages? *Answer:* It all depends. Suppose you wish to expose corruption in the police department or some other government agency, an exposure that you believe is useful in undermining public confidence in the present administration. Suppose that last year there was one conviction for bribery. Suppose that this year there have been two convictions for bribery. Instead of using total numbers, you should in this case use percentages. There has been a 100 percent increase in convictions for bribery, and heaven only knows about the unconvicted. On the other hand, if you are advertising a cold remedy that cures 2 percent of the people who use it and the major competing remedy cures 1.5 percent, then you should use the total number involved and claim that your remedy cures more people than any other remedy.

It is difficult to follow statistical reports, especially if they are long, involved, and require that the members of your audience perform mental comparisons. In order to aid the presentation of your case, it is useful to represent your statistics in the form of a graph. There is no point in using graphs if they will not help your case, so here are some rules for maximizing the presentation of evidence by graphs.

First, in order to exaggerate either the increase or decrease you wish to call to the attention of the audience, you may do one of two things: either present a graph with a missing legend, or blow up one part of the graph. Please keep in mind that at no time are we using false figures. This is purely an exercise in emphasis.

As an example, let us imagine someone trying to call attention to the increase in crime in specific areas. A true graph of the situation looks like this:

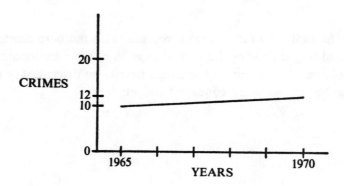

In order to highlight that increase, you might remove a legend and present the graph as follows:

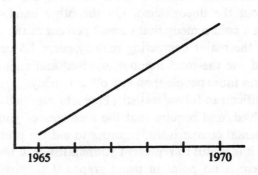

An even better graph is a blow-up to highlight the increase:

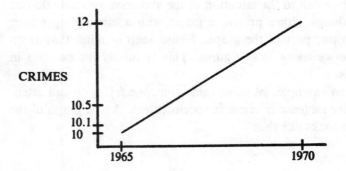

In addition to line graphs, you may also use bare charts. A special way for easing the mental anguish of your audience is to emphasize your point with cutouts. Below, we dramatically present the increase in the education budget:

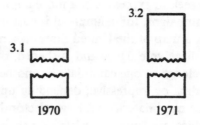

Another technique for dramatic effect is to confine measurement to one dimension and to manipulate the other dimensions. For example, an employer wishes to emphasize the increase in benefits he has extended to his employees. He shows a picture of two workers each sitting upon a pile of coins representing employee benefits before and after his conferring of benefits. The truth of the matter is that he has doubled the benefits and therefore the pile on the right is twice as high as the pile on the left. Yet, because the piles are also drawn to scale, the pile on the right is twice as wide as the pile on the left. In terms of volume, the pile on the right is four times as large even though benefits have only doubled.

A final technique that should be kept in mind for dramatizing the presentation of statistical data is the translation of the data from one medium into another. Perhaps the most common instance of this is the equation of people with geography. There is, of course, no uniform relation between the size of an area in square miles and the population density of that area. Many large geographical areas have extremely small populations whereas small geographical areas have extremely high populations. If the support for your case is not impressive in one dimension or medium, then seek to express it in a more impressive medium. In presidential campaigns, for example, it is customary for the news media to show a map of the United States wherein each state has its electoral college vote figure and is shaded, or not, in order to show that it belongs to one candidate or another. This technique can be misleading or impressive, depending upon your point of view, because a candidate with a large electoral vote may have a small geographical presentation, whereas a candidate with a large geographical backing may have a small electoral vote. The positions are further detracted from or enhanced depending upon the number of bordering states a candidate has. The more connected in space his support is the more solid it appears; the more diffuse, the less solid. The only way to overcome this imbalance if you are victimized by it is to draw the map not to geographical scale, but in proportion to electoral vote. In the latter case, Rhode Island will be bigger than Alaska. The other compensatory maneuver is to collect supporting states together not by actual borders, but by position in support, or group them alphabetically.

There has been a great deal of talk about how the middle class is always being victimized. Suppose you wanted to show that the middle class is being victimized for the benefit of the rich. One way you can do that is to *superimpose* a graph of the middle class's share of total U.S. income onto a graph that shows the share of that income possessed by the upper 20 percent (the rich class). The graph shows two things: (1) that the upper class's share is rising and the middle class's share is falling; (2) that there is a gap between the two classes.

The superimposition helps you to disguise cleverly that over a thirty year period (1950-1980) the actual share possessed by the middle class has fallen less than one-half of one percent, and the rise of the upper class share has been only one tenth of one percent. These otherwise statistically insignificant variations are lost to the eye because it only sees the "gap" at the right hand side of the graph.

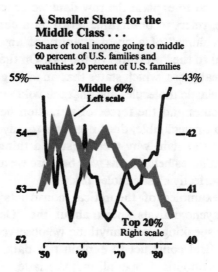

A Smaller Share for the Middle Class . . .

Share of total income going to middle 60 percent of U.S. families and wealthiest 20 percent of U.S. families

Theoretical Constructs

There are of course many ways to classify beliefs, but for our purposes it is enough to divide beliefs into two large groups: (a) raw data and (b) theory or theoretical constructs. Examples of raw data include such things as the names of people, the color of an automobile, the date, among other things. Raw data may be briefly characterized as any information that has, is, or might be checked by observation. Theoretical constructs, on the other hand, are not things one can check by simple observation. They are the product of intellectual activity and are freely used to help integrate raw data. In the previous section on statistics we discussed statistics as raw data; in this section we shall discuss theoretical constructs and their use.

Let us sharpen the distinction by seeing how theoretical constructs are most effectively used, as in the domain of physical science. Scientists distinguish between observational terms such as color, weight, pressure, and so on (which refer to observable entities), and theoretical terms such as electron, psi function, and the like (which do not refer to things we see). Theoretical constructs are used to explain the raw data we observe. Boyle's law, for example, refers to observable terms: at a constant "temperature," the "volume" of a given quantity of any gas is inversely proportional to the "pressure" of the gas. On the other hand, the theory of ideal gases, which states that an ideal gas would consist of perfectly elastic molecules and that the volume occupied by the actual molecules and the forces of attraction between the molecules is zero or negligible, does not refer to anything observable but is used to explain why there is such a thing as Boyle's law. We infer that gases behave this way because we assume that a gas consists of perfectly elastic molecules.

Other examples of theoretical constructs abound. When Freudian psychoanalysts speak about the "Oedipus complex" they are not speaking about anything we observe but are employing a theoretical construct to explain raw data. When Marxists talk about economic "imperialism," the latter expression is not something that one sees but a construct to explain what is actually seen, e.g., colonies. When historians talk about the "French Revolution" they are not referring to a single event, such as the storming of the Bastille, but rather invoking a theoretical construct to explain a whole series of events. When student radicals of the 1960s talked about the "Establishment," we realize that they were not referring to a specific person or event but offering a theory to explain a whole spectrum of events and activities.

The interesting thing about theoretical constructs is that they refer to nothing observable yet we use them to explain what we do observe. Since they refer to nothing observable they cannot literally be shown to be false. For example, if someone uses an observational term like "red," as in "your car is red," we check the truth of his statement by looking at your car. If your car is not red but blue, then his statement is false. On the other hand, there is no way of conclusively checking a theoretical construct, even in science. Although this matter is too complicated for us to go into here, we may note that if we found a gas that did not obey Boyle's law our initial reaction would be to assume that there is some obstruction or other cause or variable we have not taken into account. To have constructs that cannot be disproven in one's arsenal is to possess a deadly weapon.

Let us exemplify a theoretical construct in action. Suppose I wish to argue the case that our society is corrupt. I may invoke the theoretical construct that our society is run by a secret clique or is the victim of a superconspiracy. Suppose I am asked to produce evidence of this conspiracy. My reply is that all of my evidence has been destroyed by the people behind the conspiracy.

Another example, this time using some supporting evidence, is an argument to the effect that Lincoln never existed. Lincoln was a mythical figure invented by a group of Northern industrialists who wanted to seize control of the country. *Evidence:* The log-cabin stories are too cornball to be believed. Nobody could have written all of the beautiful speeches attributed to Lincoln; obviously they were the work of a team of speech writers. A careful examination of the portraits of Lincoln show a great series of changes over the years; just notice how his beard varies from period to period; this could only be because a number of different actors were hired to "play" the part of Lincoln. Finally, when John Wilkes Booth shot "Lincoln" he was really shooting a rival actor who got the "part" instead of him; you will notice that Booth was not caught alive but shot before he could reveal the true story behind the conspiracy. Does this sound plausible?

Let us look at a final example and then compare it to the previous ones. In a hospital for the mentally ill there is a man who claims to be dead. In an effort to bring him back to his sanity, a doctor deliberately cuts the man in order to show that the man bleeds. The doctor triumphantly turns to the patient and declares, "You must be alive, you're bleeding." The patient merely replies, "That just goes to show that dead men can sometimes bleed."

It is not likely that most audiences would accept the theory of the inmate of the insane asylum. On the other hand, conspiracies always appeal to people. The trick here is to find theoretical constructs already in use and widely accepted by your audience and to use them as if they were the same thing as raw data. Despite the fact that it has no standing among many in the scientific community, Freudian psychoanalysis has so infected the popular mind that most people, or a good many of them, literally believe in such things as the unconscious, repression, and the Oedipus complex. Generations of college students implicitly have accepted Marxist theories of history, economics, and politics even though they are not aware that these theoretical constructs are Marxist in origin. In argumentation, it is always a question of what your audience will fall for.

Classification

In addition to presenting raw data, we must classify or organize it. Theoretical constructs are just one way of organizing or classifying information. There are several others.

All and Some:

Avoid using the quantifiers "all" and "some." Do not say, "All good union members respond to strike calls"; rather say, "Good union members respond to strike calls." Why? If you do not use the word "all" you can still act as if you used the word "all" rather than the word "some." You want to avoid using "some" in your own presentation because your case will then sound too weak. The word "all," even implicitly, is much stronger sounding. At the same time, by not actually using the word you leave open the alternative of saying that you only meant to say "some," especially if your opponents challenge your statement later.

Continuum:

There are some vague classificatory terms that form part of a spectrum or continuum rather than extremes of a clear-cut division. For example, we can make a clear-cut distinction between animals with a backbone (vertebrates) and animals without backbones (invertebrates). But there is no clear-cut distinction between bald and not-bald people. How many hairs must a man have on his head in order not to be called bald? In such cases, you are at liberty to draw the line where it suits your convenience or vanity.

Obviously anyone who challenges your distinctions in such cases is a quibbler.

Golden Mean:

It is part of our general store of wisdom that the mean between two extremes is the most desirable position. Hence one should always aim to describe his position as a mean, a golden mean, between two undesirable extremes. The task here is to identify what constitutes the extremes in the minds of the audience.

In politics we have the following golden means:

The *moderate* is the mean between liberals and conservatives.
The *liberal* is the mean between radicals and reactionaries.
The *conservative* is the mean between fascists and socialists.

Even in mathematics we can find the golden mean. If there is a dispute between two parties, one of whom claims that the sum of two and two is four and another of whom claims that the sum of two and two is six, we may claim that the sum of two and two is five. Remember, people love compromises.

One final word of advice: there are an infinite number of ways in which you may classify. The only limit is your own imagination.

Definition

There is a classic point in every argument where a great outcry goes up that the participants involved should define their terms. We may call this the classical pause, and it is an important one. No one, including you, will really understand your case, if you do not know the precise sense in which you are using your terms. There are three different ways in which you should be aware of your definitions.

First, there is the case of *truth by definition.* If your terms are defined carefully enough, and if your other factual data are correct, then your case is foolproof. For example, suppose I define the term "Enlightenment" at the very beginning of my argument as a term to cover Western European writers of the eighteenth century who believed that the method of science would eventually solve all human problems. Suppose, further, that I specify exactly the geographical boundaries of Western Europe, the temporal dimension of the eighteenth century, the exact nature of the scientific method, and what I mean by a human problem. Given this definition, I examine the writings of Jean-Jacques Rousseau. I find that he fits every specification except the implicit or explicit trust in scientific methodology. Hence I may conclude that Rousseau is not an Enlightenment writer. No doubt there will be historians of ideas and others who will immediately attack my exclusion of Rousseau and they may even show how many have classified Rousseau as an Enlightenment writer. But all of this is irrelevant in the light of my definition. My position remains invincible to all such attacks. Of course one could ask what value my definition has, but although this is a legitimate question it is a totally separate question from the question of whether Rousseau is an Enlightenment writer in view of my definition.

Second, there is the matter of *equivocation*. A specific term is said to be equivocal when it has more than one meaning. For example, the term "discrimination" has a positive connotation in cases where it means being selective on the basis of certain standards. A man may be said to have discriminating taste in his choice of clothes. "Discrimination" has a negative connotation in cases where it means to deny something to someone on purely arbitrary grounds. A man is said to discriminate when he refuses to serve blacks in his restaurant. When you use equivocal terms, and there is nothing inherently wrong or even avoidable in these cases, you should be aware of the fact that the term is equivocal, and the precise sense in which you intend the term to be taken. It is sometimes advantageous to specify the exact sense in advance if there is no alternative term and if you wish to capitalize on the possible value of that particular equivocal term.

On the other hand, it is sometimes advantageous not to specify the exact sense in which you wish a term to be taken. Here your motives may be that the term has a positive connotation to everyone and you wish to capitalize on this, but at the same time you want to leave open some alternative ways of interpreting that term. Politics in general, and diplomacy in particular, require the rigid use of equivocation. Take for example the term "neutrality." The term has a positive connotation; everyone respects a neutral. But exactly what does it mean? Neutrality may mean official spoken policy as opposed to actual practice. Neutrality may mean strict nonintervention of both word and deed. Neutrality may even mean the refusal to help one side while permitting a state of affairs that by negligence helps the opposing side.

A third definitional consideration concerns the possibility of really *creative thinking* (euphemism). The advance of human knowledge requires that new concepts by invented by man. This is certainly true of the sciences, as witnessed by the importance of Newton's invention of calculus as a means for explaining motion through time. Without the invention of calculus we could not have modern physics. There is certainly no reason to discourage creativity in other realms as well.

What follows is a list of some of the most creative concepts I have come across recently. They are phrases that incorporate *(a)* a traditional term having a highly positive connotation, and *(b)* a qualification to cover new cases.

1. "genuine facsimile"—since the word "facsimile" is present, no one can claim that deception is being practiced here; at the same time, all of the value of the term "genuine" is achieved; the phrase as a whole simply means a highly detailed imitation;

2. "permanent guest artist"— of course a guest artist is not a regular or fulltime member; of course if you are permanent you are a regular or fulltime member; in fact, this is a category of special praise for someone who is otherwise a regular and fulltime member but not bound to rules that apply to others;

3. "Department of Defense"—this is a substitute for the Department of War; has anyone ever heard of declaring defense? This is a euphemism for an otherwise necessary evil and signifies,

allegedly, that the country only fights in self-defense.

4. "selective pacifism"—we all know that pacifists will not fight under any set of circumstances; but, by being selective, one leaves open the possibility of fighting when he pleases and retains all moral aura of a pacifist. Is there any way of distinguishing behaviorally, not by rhetoric, among a pacifist of the selective persuasion, a militarist, and the normal type of behavior?

5. "nonviolent force"—you may now do anything you wish to do, even employ force, but the force is accompanied by the rhetoric of appeals to nonviolence.

6. "symbolic speech"—any act of behavior, other than speaking, that is illegal or immoral may claim the protection of the first amendment on the grounds that it is symbolic speech.

7. "selective censorship"—one who appeals to this is not in favor of censorship; there are just *some* books and *some* people who ought not to be allowed public exposure. Is there a difference between this and pure unadulterated censorship?

8. "script assimilation"
(otherwise known as forgery).

9. "social subtraction'
(otherwise known as murder).

In conclusion, I should like to relate this section on definition to the section wherein I discussed gaining the sympathy of the audience. If you are going to be really creative in your thinking, then I suggest that you incorporate concepts that at least sound like the concepts you know your audience accepts. Preferably you should follow up the very concepts or ideas you appealed to in that section of presenting your case.

Analogy

When we assert an analogy, we are claiming that two things that are similar in one or more respects will be similar in another or future respect. Two things are analogous when they are similar in one or more respects. The greater the similarity the stronger will be the analogy. However, similarity is not identity. Hence there is always some point at which the analogy will break down. This is not necessarily a handicap since it is only important that the similarity holds in those respects which are relevant to what you would like to prove.

There are two kinds of analogies, literal and figurative. In a *literal* analogy we are arguing that:

> A has properties $p_1 p_2, \ldots p_n \ldots$ and p_x;
> B has properties $p_1 p_2, \ldots p_n \ldots$;
> therefore, B has the property p_n

This kind of literal analogy has been very successfully used in scientific research to construct theories. For example, Niels Bohr's theory of the atom was originally constructed along the model of the solar system (the nucleus is analogous to the sun and electrons are analogous to rotating planets, etc.). This model was later given up but it did prove to be extremely useful for a long time. In trying to discover cures for serious diseases, research scientists try to use analogies to other cures. For example, maybe cancer, like other diseases, is caused by a virus. Maybe inoculation will be a means of prevention. A map, in a sense, is analogous to the geographical area of which it is a map, although the area possesses properties that the map does not (for example, the geographical area is three dimensional while the map is usually two dimensional).

There is a difference between saying that A and B have different properties and saying that A and B have incompatible properties. When the analogy between A and B breaks down it is not because they have different properties, but rather because they have incompatible properties. For example, maps and the area described by the maps have different properties (two dimensions as opposed to three dimensions). However, it is conceivable that we can have a three dimensional map. On the other hand, there is an incompatibility between methadone and a vitamin pill. Methadone is a synthetic heroin substitute used to treat addicts. Despite all of its benefits, methadone is addictive whereas a vitamin pill is not, even though both are analogously preventing something. Here the analogy suffers a serious incompatibility and breakdown. In short, before using a literal analogy make sure that there is no incompatibility with the major point you are trying to prove.

Figurative (illustrative) analogies are not meant to show literal similarities and structures or functions. Rather, they are literary devices for dramatically exemplifying a point. If you use figurative analogies you should make sure that the analogy is definitely positive and favorable to your case. At the same time, the analogy should reinforce the kind of sympathy-appealing devices you used in the first part of your presentation. At all times the predisposition of the audience should be kept in mind.

An example of a figurative analogy that is, at the same time, an example of an *ad populum* appeal is the so-called "ship-of-state." You should also note in the following examples the extent to which a clever person can take the same metaphor of a ship-of-state and come out with a different conclusion.

1. Thomas Carlyle: "Running a government is like running a ship; we need a strong hand at the helm."

2. Henrik Ibsen: "Society is like a ship; everyone must be prepared to take the helm."

3. Alexis de Tocqueville: "Like the navigator he [the statesman] may direct the vessel which bears him along but he can neither change its structure nor raise the winds nor lull the waters which swell beneath him."

4. J. M. Beck: "The constitution is neither, on the one hand, a Gibraltar Rock, which wholly resists the ceaseless washing of time and circumstance, nor is it, on the other hand, a sandy beach which is slowly destroyed by the erosions of the waves. It is rather to be likened to a floating dock, which, while firmly attached to its moorings, and not therefore at the caprice of the waves, yet rises and falls with the tide of time and circumstances."

Another figurative analogy that is, at the same time, a way of reinforcing the appeal to pity is the analogy between crime and disease. In his book *Erewhon,* which is "nowhere" misspelled backwards, Samuel Butler both satirizes Victorian England and argues that any distinction between crime and disease is ridiculous. In *Erewhon* anyone who commits a crime is "cured," whereas anyone who becomes ill, say a person who contracts tuberculosis, is punished.

> This is what I gathered. That in that country if a man falls into ill health, or catches any disorder, or fails bodily in any way before he is seventy years old, he is tried before a jury of his countrymen, and if convicted is held up to public scorn and sentenced more or less severely as the case may be. There are subdivisions of illness into crimes and misdemeanors as with offenses amongst ourselves—a man being punished very heavily for serious illness, while failure of eyes or hearing in one over sixty-five, who has had good health hitherto, is dealt with by fine only, or imprisonment in default of payment. But if a man forges a cheque, or sets his house on fire, or robs with violence from the person, or does any other such things as are criminal in our own country, he is either taken to a hospital and most carefully tended at public expense, or if he is in good circumstances, he lets it be known to all his friends that he is suffering from a severe fit of immorality. . . . Bad conduct . . . is nevertheless held to be the result of either pre-natal or post-natal misfortune . . . . The judge said that he acknowledged the probable truth, namely, that the prisoner was born of unhealthy parents, or had been starved in infancy, or had met with some accidents which had developed consumption . . . he knew all of this, and regretted that the protection of society obliged him to inflict additional pain. . . . The judge was fully persuaded that the infliction of pain upon the weak and sickly was the only means of preventing weakness and sickness from spreading, and that ten times the suffering inflicted upon the accused was eventually warded off from others by the present apparent severity. I could therefore perfectly understand his inflicting whatever pain he might consider necessary in order to prevent so bad an example from spreading further and lowering the Erewhinian standard; but it seemed almost childish to tell the prisoner that he could have been in good health, if he had been more fortu-

nate in his constitution, and been exposed to less hardships when he was a boy.

An example of a provocative analogy that might conceivably serve as either a literal or a figurative analogy is the one between Marxism and Christianity. As far as I know, Bertrand Russell was the first to call attention to the parallels in his *History of Western Philosophy:*

> To understand Marx psychologically, one should use the following dictionary:
>
> | | | |
> |---:|:---:|:---|
> | Yahweh | = | Dialectical Materialism |
> | The Messiah | = | Marx |
> | The Elect | = | The Proletariat |
> | The Church | = | The Communist Party |
> | The Second Coming | = | The Revolution |
> | Hell | = | Punishment of the Capitalists |
> | The Millenium | = | The Communist Commonwealth |
>
> The terms on the left give the emotional content of the terms on the right, and it is this emotional content, familiar to those who have had a Christian or a Jewish upbringing, that makes Marx's eschatology credible. . . .

Lewis Feuer has used this same analogy and even extended it a bit: ". . . . like other creeds, it has its sacred text, its saints, its heretics, its elect, its holy city. If Marx was its Messiah, Lenin was its Saint Paul."

DRIVING HOME THE CONCLUSION

The point you are trying to make, the case you are presenting, must be epitomized in the conclusion. Everything you have done up until now has just been preparation for the conclusion. First, you have tried to gain the implicit trust of the audience; second, you have presented data for the express purpose of backing up your conclusion. Naturally you should have had your conclusion in mind when selecting the information to present. The question we raise now is how and in what form that conclusion should be presented.

There are certain key words and phrases that not only signify to the audience that you are drawing the conclusion but, at the same time, reinforce in the minds of the members of the audience that your conclusion is the right one. The following key words and phrases should be used profusely when stating the conclusion:

1. obviously
2. certainly
3. there is no question that . . .
4. of course
5. surely
6. it is clearly evident that . . .

Evidence and conclusion are related to each other in at least one of two ways. Either the conclusion is a specific instance and the evidence consists of generalizations under which the specific instance falls, *or* the conclusion is a generalization and the evidence consists of specific instances that support the conclusion.

Let us look at the first possibility:

general ⟶ specific.

In arguing for a conclusion about something specific—lets say the prohibition of marijuana—we may appeal to the generalizaton that all drugs are or should be prohibited unless given under medical supervision. Another example would be the justification of rebelling against the present administration or the government of the United States by appeal to the precedent (here serving as a generalization) of revolution in American life. Here one claims kinship with Patrick Henry and John Hancock. Once your audience has accepted certain generalizations, which you presented in the first two parts of your presentation, they must accept the conclusion.

Let us now examine the second possibility:

specific   ━━━━━▶   general

Statistical evidence is more often than not an example of going from specific cases to a general conclusion. Political polls of voter opinion are now frequently used as justifications for making policy decisions for the whole country. In fact, one might argue that elections are simply crucial polls.

There are other examples. Suppose I form an all-star basketball team made up of individuals who are acknowledged to be the greatest players. I choose Larry Bird, Magic Johnson, Charles Barkley, Okham Olyanion, and Michael Jordan. From these specific stars I might conclude that the team as a whole will be a star team or a great team.

As a final example, let us imagine two opponents each trying to argue for the same general conclusion: how to prevent war, any war. One side argues that the arms race or the stockpiling of weapons has always preceded a major war. Hence, if we do not have an arms race we shall not have a war. The other side argues that the lack of military preparedness on one side incites aggression in others. It even produces as evidence the same debate in England in the 1930s where, much to their later chagrin, many prominent people argued against a military buildup. Hence, preparedness is the only way to prevent war. Both sides are appealing to different specific examples.

It is, of course, possible to defend a position or a conclusion by using both general and specific information. In fact, the strongest arguments usually have this double-barreled kind of support. Suppose we want to defend the conclusion that prostitution ought to be legalized. We might appeal to the general principle of free enterprise, which encourages everyone to compete in an open market and offer any product or service he can to the public. By not having legalized prostitution (with medical supervision) we are encouraging an illegal monopoly on the part of the Mafia or others. Moreover, and here we appeal to specific statistical evidence, aids is killing more and more people every year.

In the initial presentation, only positive evidence should be presented on behalf of your case. Other kinds of support will be considered later when we discuss rebuttals. In addition to achieving one end, any means or course we pursue is bound to have other consequences. Any rational person considers *all* of the consequences before selecting a specific remedy. This truth is of great value in the presentation of an argument. In addition to presenting evidence for why your position or point of view is correct, there is no reason in the world why you should not point out the residual benefits of your solution. In fact, a long list of residual benefits frequently serves as the deciding factor.

To begin with, act as if your solution had only positive residual benefits. Second, know what problems outside of the one under discussion are most on the minds of the audience. Third, claim that each and every one of these major problems will also be solved or at the very least ameliorated by adopting your position on the specific issue discussed. Although this tactic may cause some shock and surprise, I maintain that the only limitation on this procedure is your imagination.

Let us consider some examples. Suppose I am arguing against the use of marijuana and in favor of strong laws prohibiting its distribution and use. I might add as a residual benefit that the generation gap is caused by or exacerbated by the use of marijuana. Adopt my solution and you solve both problems. Even the cold war can be defrosted if our youth are clear-headed, and they can only be clear-headed if they are not smoking pot.

Now let me argue for the legal use of marijuana. Legalize pot, and even encourage parents to smoke it rather than drinking alcoholic beverages, and you will bring the generations together. Moreover, if everyone sat around smoking pot and making love, no one would ever feel aggressive enough to want to make war.

The real clincher to any conclusion is the use of *emotion language,* either positively toward what you favor or negatively toward what you oppose. If you are absolutely sure that your audience is with you, then you can wrap up your presentation by simply restating your conclusion in emotive terminology.

Consider the following summation presented to a Southern jury by Matt Murphy in defense of a white man being tried for murder:

> And this white woman who got killed? White woman? Where's that NAACP card? I thought I'd never see the day when Communists and niggers and white niggers and Jews were flying under the banner of the United Nations flag, not the American flag we fought for. . . . I'm proud to be a white man and I'm proud that I stand up on my feet for white supremacy. Not black supremacy; not the mixing and mongrelization of races . . . not the Zionists that run that bunch of niggers. The white people are not gonna run before them. And when white people join up to 'em they become white niggers. . . .

The substance of Mr. Murphy's plea is quite simple even if controversial. He and therefore his client are of a certain ideology and the slain woman was of an opposed ideology. Further, he believes that the audience shares his client's ideology and will therefore excuse the act, which is never denied. Yet it is the way in which this content is conveyed rather than the content itself that is all important.

That different statements can convey, at least minimally, the same information but with different connotations or emotional impact is best exemplified in another Bertrand Russell quotation, the conjugation of firmness: "I am firm; you are obstinate; he is pig-headed."

Newspaper headlines, not just the editorials, are also slanted emotionally and are frequently designed to be that way. I have in mind one event the facts of which I will not convey. Rather I simply repeat the headlines from different newspapers and let the reader decide what he thinks happened:

STATE TROOPERS GUN DOWN STUDENTS

TWO STUDENTS SHOT IN GUNFIRE EXCHANGE WITH POLICE

MURDER ON CAMPUS
COPS FORCED TO KILL IN SELF-DEFENSE

NONVERBAL DEVICES

The discussion of emotive terminology leads naturally to a discussion of the other subliminal devices of which one must be aware in presenting an argument. As Marshall McLuhan never tires of repeating, the medium is the message. Here again, your assessment of the audience is crucial. What preconceptions do they have that you wish to use? Find out what these are and the nonverbal devices are obvious.

For example, clothing is important. A boy was arrested for the possession of marijuana. The boy had a Mohawk haircut and was wearing black leather clothing with spikes when arrested. By the time his trial hearing came up his entire appearance had changed: short haircut and Brooks Brothers suit.

In oral presentation, voice is important. Your voice must be sincere and confident, but above all it must be deep. Absolutely everyone I know is impressed by a deep voice and there are even exercises you can perform to deepen your voice. Facial expressions and eye movements are also important in this respect. The general rule here is to look people straight in the eye and never have shifty eyes. People with shifty eyes are automatically considered devious whereas any man who looks you straight in the eye must be honest.

The nature of the room or general surroundings are also important. I have heard a story to the effect that former FBI director J. Edgar Hoover stood on a raised platform behind his desk when meeting an agent for the first time. The principle implied seems to be that height adds stature as well, and it is true that we are impressed by tall men.

The Prussian chancellor Otto Bismarck had a great reputation for diplomacy. He frequently victimized lesser men (lesser from a chemical point of view) by insisting upon serving champagne throughout negotiations. Part of his secret was his ability to consume large amounts of alcohol without losing control of himself or the situation.

The most accomplished use of surroundings I know of is in the work of Evangelist Billy Graham. The large public places were he speaks are decorated with flowers and flags, his audiences primed by singing and other means until they slowly reach a crescendo for his own talk.

Not to be forgotten in any discussion of nonverbal techniques is the use of technological innovations. The latest and most effective seems to be video tape and cassettes. The great advantages of video tape are that it can be edited for maximum effect and you cannot cross-examine a tape. The latter is especially important if your tape has the currently fashionable quasidocumentary style. The only way you can counter this is with another tape edited to show your point of view.

Examples of the use of film abound. The French director Godard seems obsessed with using the medium solely for propaganda purposes. In the 1964 Democratic National Convention, a film was shown depicting a little girl playing with a flower, quickly followed by an atomic explosion. The film was directed against Barry Goldwater, the Republican candidate.

ADVERTISING AS A CASE STUDY

In advertising we find many of the techniques discussed above developed into a fine art. Especially instructive is advertising's almost complete reliance upon *positive* argument. Let us follow the foregoing outline and see to what extent advertising exemplifies each of the principles.

To begin with, the advertiser must identify his market, break it down into its meaningful components (e.g., geography, age, sex, and so on), and the objectives he hopes to achieve in his advertising. Second, he must identify his product with the dual hope of (1) explaining the product in terms of the consumers' wants and needs, and (2) emphasize the individuality or superiority of his product over rival products. It is important to note, however, that the latter must be done in a subtle manner.

Gaining a sympathetic audience:

In the case of advertising this means creating a conscious or felt need for the product.

a) *appeal to pity:* This works in two ways in advertising: either directly for the product or service, or indirectly through pity for those who need the product. As an example of the first kind we may note the Avis car rental commercials and advertisements that call attention to the *fact* that Avis is only number 2 (Hertz is first) and as a result has to try harder. Here the appeal to pity is an appeal to the American sympathy for the underdog. As an example of the second kind, we may note advertisements for exercise programs for ninety-pound weaklings and our sympathy for them is extended to any product attempting to help them cope with a cruel world.

b) *appeal to authority:* This has to be either the first or second most prominent device used in the world of advertising. Examples are incredibly numerous. One patent medicine designed to relieve headaches and various other assorted ills notes that it contains more of the ingredient most recommended by doctors. Whatever that ingredient is, the mere fact that it is recommended by someone in a position of authority, namely the doctor or doctors, makes this an appeal to authority. Several toothpastes have a "kind" of endorsement from the American Dental Association. For those who are too cynical about medical authority or for those who are not sophisticated enough to care, there is always the vitamin-enriched bread endorsed by the famous athlete.

c) *appeal to tradition:* There are several interesting variations on this theme. First, we all know the name of Napoleon's favorite brandy, and if the Napoleonic legend is something that appeals to you, then so will this brandy—which happens to be good in spite of Napoleon. Closer to home is Dolly Madison ice cream. Now I do not know the exact connection between Dolly Madison (wife of President James Madison) and this product. It is true that

Dolly Madison was the first to make ice cream in America. But what exactly does this imply?

The latest and most impressive use of an appeal to tradition, the attempt to show that one's product is consistent with a generally accepted ideal, is at the same time a factual appeal. Detergents are now chemically produced so that they do not pollute our waters. The early advertising for these products was not only an appeal to a traditional value but a very subtle way of noting the superiority of one product over another. Without some form of advertising most of us would never know this fact.

As a final example, I note that some products have a union label attached to them so that anyone who is favorably disposed to unions may choose that product over its rivals. Current interest in buying American-made products is another example. Who would want to be accused of not supporting American goods?

(d) *appeal to precedent:* The advertising counter-part to an appeal to precedent is the testimonial. Of course the testimonial is also an appeal to authority. If I can present letters of gratitude or interviews expressing enthusiasm for a product by people who sincerely claim that the product fulfilled their needs, then I have established precedents for your thinking that the product will help you. Here it is important that the precedents be like the potential purchaser. A celebrity is an appeal to authority. That means that famous people are out in a strict appeal to precedent and that the common man or the "housewife" are to be favored. For example, Oleg Cassini no doubt sends his shirts to a top commercial laundry, or maybe he does not have to wear the same one twice. On the other hand, John Doe, who can only afford to own two dress shirts, has a wife who is interested in a bleach that will get the yellow stains out of his shirt collars. Hence Mrs. Doe is more interested in a precedent (testimonial) from Mrs. Smith or Jones.

Presenting the facts:

In advertising this means providing support for the contention that your product satisfies the need you have aroused in the previous part of your presentation.

a) *statistics:* What mother has not waited for her son to run home and say, "Look Mom, no cavities," or, "Look Mom, 40 percent fewer cavities." There are several toothpastes that can present documentary evidence of statistical surveys showing that their product is superior in preventing tooth decay. Again, we have seen the bandwagon approach used often in advertising. If more people use Product A than any of its rivals, then clearly you should be using it too. We are also very familiar with the use of graphs. We know that Listerine kills more germs faster because we have actually seen the graph in action on television.

There is an important variation of the theme of *accentuating the positive.* We may all view a product from a different point of view. Hence, if your product possesses a property that others think to be undesirable, you must reconstruct their world view so that they come to see that what you lack is no shortcoming and that what you have is an asset. For example, for a long time the Volkswagen did not have automatic transmission. Rather than admit that this was a shortcoming, they advertised from the point of view that standard gear shifts were really the greatest, and what "man" would want his car to drive him rather than vice versa? Further, anyone who has ever used contact paper, which is very useful, knows that in time it stretches. Rather than admit this, the company advertised that its product did not shrink. It all depends on how you look at it.

As a result of growing concern over the relationship between the presence of cholesterol and the occurrence of heart attacks and strokes, the beef industry has been busy both in trying to develop lower cholesterol beef and in some creative advertising. With regard to the latter, it has initiated an advertising campaign that has two dimensions. First, it emphasizes that one of the residual benefits of eating beef is greater strength because it contains protein, iron, and B vitamins. Moreover, it has initiated a series of ads stating that "Beef has only 76 milligrams of cholesterol in a three-ounce serving" and that a healthy person can consume up to 300 milligrams a day. What the ads do not tell you is that the piece of beef in question was surgically trimmed with every iota of fat removed and, moreover, that the average serving the consumer eats weighs five ounces.

The actual information provided by the beef industry is correct. What it leaves out is quite clearly crucial to the consumer. What is important for our purposes is that the advertising campaign instances the use of correct information to create or influence attitudes, but these attitudes would be very different if other information were also available. It is not a matter of lying that interests us but the presentation of information.

b) *classification:* The important thing in classifying your product or products is to make sure that the classification is laudatory. For example, in my neighborhood delicatessen there are two sizes of precooked chickens: large and extra large. There is no such entity as a small or medium chicken. Another example of this kind of classification is found in eggs. Did you know that it is impossible to get a small egg? The smallest egg sold commercially is sold as a medium egg.

c) *definition:* Suppose you were to read the word "champagne" on a bottle of wine. What would that tell you? To some people it means a wine from the Champagne region of France. Technically this is all that it means. Further, most of the wine from this region is sparkling, which means that bubbles form within it. Moreover, most of this wine is white. However, there are wines from the Champagne region that are red and some that are not sparkling. French champagne is rigidly produced and controlled, especially its labeling. An example of this is the fact that it is bottle fermented: the bubbles are allowed to form naturally in the bottle and not pumped in by some artificial device. This produces the best taste, but it is also very costly.

In America the law allows certain products to use the word "champagne," but the requirements are so loose that it is easy to buy an inferior product. A good many American champagnes are fermented not in the bottle, but in huge vats. If the champagne is vat fermented it must say "bulk process" on the label.

However, this does not prevent some unscrupulous concern from saying "naturally fermented by bulk process." The word "natural" is almost a contradiction here, but the unscrupulous concern relies on the equivocation of meaning and the buyer's natural gullibility.

d) *analogy:* This is a widely used technique. It will be useful to recall our previous distinction between literal and figurative analogies. A literal analogy is a claim that if two things are alike in one or more respects, then they are alike in some further respect. A figurative analogy is just a dramatic device for emphasizing or explaining one point. A good deal of advertising relies upon the obscurity over this distinction. What are figurative analogies are presented as literal analogies. An American sports-type car, which is relatively inexpensive, is called the Ferrari of American cars. Ferrari is a prestigious automobile that is both expensive and a masterpiece of technology. It may be that the only similarity (and certainly not an analogy) between the Ferrari and the American car is some slight styling feature. Yet advertising capitalizes on this.

Another American automobile claims to be quieter inside than a Rolls Royce. This is probably true, but that is probably the beginning and the end of any superiority.

Driving home the conclusion:

Advertising does not rely upon complicated arguments. Its stock in trade is repetition. Of the devices it employs under this general head the most important are emotive language and the promise of residual benefits.

a) *residual benefits:* In his book *The Hidden Persuaders,* Vance Packard emphasizes the subliminal promise that goes along with each product. As one man put it, "The cosmetic manufacturers are not selling lanolin, they are selling hope. . . . We do not buy just an auto, we buy prestige." Although a bit overemphasized, there is a real point here. If a man does not feel the need for an automobile it is not likely that you will sell him one. On the other hand, given man's nature, the market for automobiles, and competitors that are very similar technically to your product, some residual benefit must be offered. So you say that anyone can buy a car of Brand X but if someone buys your brand or make he not only gets a car but he gets a symbol of virility as well. The connection between cars and sex cannot just be invented by advertisers, there must already be some connection in the minds of the audience. Sociologically we may note that this particular connection between cars and sex is the result of the fact that courtship habits have changed a great deal over the past fifty years precisely because of the existence of cars.

The greatest example of emotive language, so clever that it is almost unbelievable, is an advertisement not for any specific product, but for "Brand Names." It simply says you can rely upon Brand Names. Here you are being conditioned to respond to advertising itself or to conditioning itself. Amazing!

Some brands have actually achieved a kind of superstatus. Scotch tape is not just a brand in the popular mind, but has become the generic term used by consumers of cellophane tape. The same is true of kleenex in the case of facial tissue. With such emotive status it is unlikely that competitors will have any chance. We can all learn a great deal from advertising.

Five

Attacking an Argument

There are two main reasons for learning techniques of attacking arguments. First, one can build a stronger case for his own position if, in addition to presenting positive considerations for it, he shows that there are serious weaknesses in the arguments for its rivals. Remember, in this connection, that few positions of practical importance can be *conclusively proved;* thus, while you are not likely to be able to *prove* your own position, you can make it look very good indeed by punching holes in the arguments of the opposition.

Second, once you have mastered the art of offense you will undoubtedly become more sophisticated in defense of your original position. Anticipating what and where the attacks against you will originate and how they might progress is half the battle.

AUDIENCE REACTION

For the sake of discussion we shall assume that someone else has already presented his case and now you are called upon to attack it. Before you do anything else you *must* gauge audience reaction to the original presentation of your opponent's case. There are three possible reactions: (1) either your opponent has been successful in varying degrees in persuading the audience to adopt his point of view; or (2) the audience remains undecided; or (3) your opponent has been unsuccessful in varying degrees in getting the audience to accept his case.

Let us discuss general strategy with respect to these three possibilities, reversing the order of consideration. If your opponent has been unsuccessful, the first thing you must do is to pinpoint precisely those spots in his presentation that were the weakest and least successful with the audience. Then concentrate most of your fire on these spots, thereby reinforcing in the minds of the audience the weakness of his position and your brilliance in sharing their perceptiveness. Here you are combining a critique of the opposition with flattery of the audience. Next, when you feel that the audience is with you, you may proceed to employ the techniques and rules to be discussed below and you may do so with humor and ridicule. Please note: *humor and ridicule are effective* against an opponent *only if you know yourself to be preeminent* in the eyes of the present audience. Otherwise you will offend all concerned.

There are two special devices that should be used in a blatant manner in those cases where you are sure your opponent has been unsuccessful. These devices are the *ad hominem* attack and the genetic fallacy.

Ad hominem:

To attack *ad hominem* is to attack the man who presents an argument rather than the argument itself. There are some subtle variations of it that you will discover throughout this chapter, but here we are concerned only with its more blatant use. There are two occasions during a discussion when you may use it: either after you have demolished the argument by independent means, or in those cases where your opponent's argument has been so unsuccessful with the audience that it is not worth demolishing. This is important. There are no doubt, as you shall see, all sorts of clever things you can do, but these things should be done only if needed to win. If you can win without using a technique, do not use it. You may distract both yourself and the audience.

There are various ways of attacking a man. You might begin by chastising him for insulting the intelligence of the audience by offering such a shabby case. Or you may explain why he has adopted such a foolish view.

Examples of *ad hominem* include the following. When asked to debate a particular subject with his students, a teacher may reply that he does not discuss such serious matters with a bunch of ignoramuses. Or a speaker invited to the campus by students may refuse to answer the questions of his academic audience by noting that they have not read a particular writer or have not read a particular book or magazine article.

The point of *ad hominem* is to discredit the opposition in indirect ways. One way of doing this is to call attention to infelicities in your opponents use of the English language. That is, if there are errors in grammer, diction, or just poor choice of metaphors (or the mixing of metaphors) call attention to this. The implication is that if a person mixes his meatphors then his mind must be in a state of confusion, and if his mind is confused then we do not have to take him seriously.

One should be careful with this tactic because members of the audience sometimes make such errors and they would be offended if you claim that a mixed metaphor shows a position to be invalid. However, you can present these exposures in a humorous vein and both expose inadequacies and gain the sympathy of the audience.

One traditional error is called *amphiboly,* and it is the result of sentence structure. For example, there is the famous case of the pharmacist who had a sign in his window that read "We dispense with accuracy." Would you trust a pharmacist to fill your prescription if he did not know how to express his thoughts clearly? Even more famous examples come from the Delphic oracle, which advised King Croesus when he inquired whether he should invade the neighboring kingdom that "If Croesus goes to war, he would destroy a mighty kingdom." Croesus did go to war, lost, and thereby destroyed his own kingdom. Or consider the prediction in the Shakespearean play *Macbeth* directed to Macbeth himself in which it is said "None of woman born shall harm you." Macbeth, of course, was killed by Macduff, who was born by caesarean section.

Genetic fallacy:

The most sophisticated form of *ad hominem* is a special kind of counterargument itself, namely, the genetic fallacy. To explain genetically is to describe the origin of an event, process, thing, or what have you. It is a kind of historical account of how things got that way. Usually it is employed in a diagnostic manner, thereby implying that you are discussing the case history of a disease. Genetic explanations are certainly valid and useful in other contexts, but they are especially useful in undermining an opponent.

Perhaps the two most famous uses of genetic explanation are Freudian psychoanalysis and various forms of Marxism. The anxieties, neuroses, and psychoses of many patients are identified as the result of a course of development that began in childhood. Usually some traumatic experience in childhood is the cause of the neurosis. For example, being locked in a closet as punishment might "cause" claustrophobia, or being inculcated with the view that sex is dirty might "cause" one to be frigid or impotent or require elaborate masochistic devices to relieve sexual tension. Marxists can explain, so they claim, not only the history of economic development, but why it exhibits certain patterns, such as boom and bust, and why some workers feel alienated in the capitalist system. In addition, both Freudians and Marxists can explain why some people do not accept their theories. Anyone who refuses to see that sex is all pervasive reveals a symptom of Victorian sexual repression. Perhaps he has an Oedipus complex and seeks to hide it by denying its existence in anyone. Anyone who denies that he is exploited is a tool of capitalist repression. To oppose such theories is to expose oneself to public scorn in some circles.

Genetic explanations abound in common popular argumentation. The contempt of the business world for the academic world is explained as the awareness that "those who can, do; those who cannot, teach." The contempt of the academic world for the business world is explained as the awareness that business is based on greed instead of benevolence. Adolescents simply cannot speak to anyone over twenty-five. Age functions here as a genetic explanation of political, social, and cultural blindness. All rebellious youth are to be dismissed as the result of permissive parents. Given a sympathetic audience, you can always find some explanation as to why the opposition is so stupid and save yourself the trouble of having to deal logically with its arguments.

We come now to the second possibility, namely, where the audience is still undecided. Here you should avoid using most of the techniques mentioned above. Instead you should once more try to discover which points in your opponent's presentation were strongest and which were weakest. If you can combat the strong ones, then do so; if not, simply act as if they were never mentioned. In any case, the weak points should be exploited. The exact anatomy of proceeding to do so will be discussed shortly.

The third possibility is what to do if your opponent has been successful. To begin with, *moral posturing* calculated to shame your opponent and audience is *very effective when you are the obvious underdog* in a dispute. Now if your opponent's success is owing to *his* use of techniques of deception, such as those we are discussing, you can probably win points by exposing this fact and accusing him (more or less gently) of being a trickster. But if your audience is so dimwitted that it would not see what you are driving at, you should stick to using the deceptive tricks yourself. Above all, do not be so harsh with your opponent as to increase the audience's sympathy for him, and do not give the appearance yourself of being crafty or nit-picking. Most audiences immediately dislike someone who seems impressed with his ability to argue, so avoid looking oppressively flashy or pleased with your incisiveness or wit. Strive to look like a slightly wounded, unjustly used underdog, but again, don't overdo it. Know your audience!

If your audience is somewhat sophisticated, but perhaps taken in by your opponent's skillful presentation, then you should expose him as a sophist and a trickster who is insulting the intelligence of the audience. You then engage in a point by point critique of his tricks. Finally, after the exposé you claim that you *shall not stoop* to using such dishonest means.

ANATOMY OF REFUTATION

We come now to the anatomy of refutation, the means whereby we undermine the case of the opposition. Remember, all of your opponent's arguments can be shown to be defective. It is simply a question of your ingenuity and persistence. I shall begin by diagramming the form of attack, exemplify some of the diagram's general principles, and then launch into a detailed analysis of specific refutation procedures.

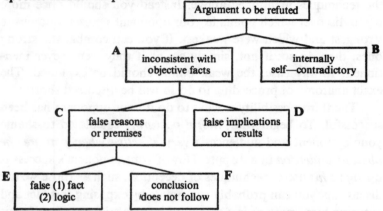

Every argument consists of a major point or conclusion supported by premises or reasons that allegedly provide evidence for the conclusion. When attacking an argument, we are claiming one of two things, or perhaps both: an argument is defective (1) when the evidence contradicts the conclusion, or (2) when the evidence is simply false or inadequate. Since *A* above will be subdivided, let us examine *B* first.

B: An argument is internally self-contradictory either when one of the premises contradicts the conclusion or when the premises contradict each other.

One of the classic cases of exposing a contradiction occurs in Plato's dialogue *Euthyphro*. Recall that a contradiction exists when the speaker makes two statements both of which cannot be true at the same time. Socrates asks Euthyphro: What is the meaning of the term "piety"? Euthyphro answers that an act is pious when the gods approve of it and impious when the gods disapprove of it. Socrates then points out to Euthyphro that since there are many gods (Greek mythology) and since some gods will approve of an act and some gods will disapprove of the same act, then the same act will be both approved and disapproved at the same time. Therefore, if we use Euthyphro's definition of piety the same act will be both pious and impious at the same time. Euthyphro, clearly, has contradicted himself.

A: An argument may be inconsistent with objective fact when either the premises or reasons appealed to are simply false *(C)*, or the implications or results of the conclusion would be considered false *(D)*. An example of the latter would be an argument that begins with information about industrial pollution and then concludes with a condemnation of all technology as being harmful to life. The false implications of this position are apparent in that a great deal of modern medicine, which preserves and serves life, is the result of technology. Surely we would not want to reject this when making such a blanket condemnation.

C: Reasons or premises are false or unacceptable either when the conclusion does not follow *(F)*, or when we can simply show the premises to be false *(E)*. In the case of *F* we say the argument is a *non sequitur*. This differs from the case of *B* because in *B* we have a contradiction, whereas in the case of *F* there is no connection at all. For example, one may argue to the conclusion that Americans as a whole have greater innate intelligence now than they did forty years ago because there are more Americans attending college now than ever before. To do so is to offer a reason that is true but totally irrelevant to the conclusion. There is no direct connection between innate intelligence and attendance at a college. The colleges may ahve lowered their standards or expanded facilities for reasons that have nothing to do with the intelligence of applicants.

E: A reason or premise can be seen to be false in either a direct or indirect way. In a direct way, if someone claims that it is raining we might show that he is wrong directly by looking outside. A reason or promise may be shown to be false indirectly in a number of ways.

Let us consider the argument that eighteen-year-olds should be allowed to drink alcohol. Let us further suppose that the sole reason or premise offered is that liability to the draft should be the sole determining factor in giving the right to drink. Usually it is stated in some highly emotional form like "we're old enough to die for our country but not old enough to drink."

The first way of attacking this premise is to (1) add another premise that is known to be true, and (2) then derive a false conclusion. Obviously this invalidates the premise. For example, girls are not subject to the draft so we would have to exclude them from drinking. Obviously being subject to the draft cannot be the sole determinant in arriving at a socially acceptable drinking age.

The second way of attacking this premise is to derive another conclusion that would be inconsistent with the given conclusion or some other conclusion that your opponent may draw. For example, if the draft age were lowered to sixteen, then sixteen-year-olds (or twelve-year-olds, or whatever the draft age is) would have the right to drink. But your opponent has argued that drinking should begin at age eighteen. The same sort of inconsistent conclusion would work with a voluntary army. Then no one but the volunteers would have the right to drink.

F: A third general method of attacking this premise is to show that it is a generalization with known exceptions, hence it is unacceptable. Liability to the draft is no present criterion for drinking since men over thirty-five, who are obviously not subject to the draft, have the right to drink. Drinking, then, depends on some other criterion or criteria. All of this is not to say that eighteen-year-olds should not have the right to drink. The refutation only shows that liability to the draft is not the premise or reason that can be used.

In general, assumptions can be attacked in one of three ways: either the assumptions overlook, evade, or distort certain facts.

We *overlook facts* when we fail to note that there are exceptions to certain rules; when we use one rule in a situation in which another rule is more applicable; when we engage in sweeping generalizations (and claim that what is true in some cases is true in all cases); when we make hasty generalizations (insufficient basis for a generalization); or when we insufficiently bifurcate an issue. In the case of the latter we set up alternatives that might not be exclusive. For example, the statement that "you are either with me or against me" is a case where the alternatives are not so exclusive. Sometimes we see this kind of argument in the claim that either you are in favor of affirmative action in the form of quotas or you are unwilling to fight discrimination. Clearly there is another alternative, namely, the desire to adopt anti-discrimination measures that do not in themselves engage in reverse discrimination.

We *evade facts* in our assumptions when we beg the question (i.e., reasserting our original position instead of supplying additional support), when we engage in special pleading, or when we are guilty of the fallacy of the complex question (i.e., argue a different issue). For an example of the latter, consider someone who says "Okay, let's discuss national defense. Shall we spend more on missiles or shall we spend more on conventional forces?" The original question might be whether we should spend, more, less, or the same, but the reply assumes that we have already agreed to spend more.

We *distort facts* in our assumptions when we use false and misleading analogies ("register all matches and prevent forest fires"), when we identify false causes (e.g., all wars in the twentieth century fought by the U.S. have been under Democratic administrations), or when we propose an irrelevant thesis as a red herring (see below).

Refutation of Pity Appeals

The appeal to pity, like the appeals to authority, *ad populum,* and precedents, is largely an attempt to gain the sympathy of the audience. If any of these appeals has been successful, then it is important to realize that the audience has a certain sympathy for that kind of argument. Hence the refutation follows one of two patterns: either we invoke a higher order appeal of the same nature, or we attempt to turn the tables.

If your opponent has appealed to pity, then you should act as if his example of pity is a general premise. Then add some premise of your own that you think would be accepted by the audience and derive a conclusion which is inconsistent with that of your opponent. For example, suppose your opponent has argued that we should destroy all atomic weapons, and has begun his argument with a detailed survey of the consequences of Hiroshima. Further, we suppose the appeal to pity to have been an effective one. The audience obviously feels pity for those who suffer. The only way to counter this appeal is to point out that if America had not possessed or used atomic weapons on Japan (as your opponent argues), and if the war had had to be concluded by an invasion of the Japanese islands, then (adding the supplementary premise) by the best estimates the casualties on both sides, including military and civilian, would have been astronomical. Now add: How many Japanese and American children and their parents are alive because of that courageous decision to drop the bomb? The use of atomic weapons actually minimized suffering.

As a second example, imagine a lawyer defending a juvenile client by claiming that *because* his client is a child, *therefore* we ought to make allowances. The appeal to pity has the following structure: because of *x*, therefore *y*.

We turn the tables by deriving a different conclusion from the same premise: because of *x*, therefore not *y*. Because he is a child, we ought not to make allowances, otherwise we shall be establishing or encouraging a bad habit.

Refutation of Authority

There are two ways of undermining your opponent's use of authority, either by an *ad hominem* attack on his specific authorities, or by providing counter-authorities. Further, there are at least six different kinds of *ad hominem* attacks upon an authority.

First, if a man is quoted as an authority and at the same time is known to have opinions that are inconsistent with the appeals to pity, *ad populum,* or precedent used by your opponent, then you should pounce upon this inconsistency. Let us go back to a previous example. If your opponent has argued against the stockpiling of nuclear weapons, and has further exemplified his case by the pity appeal of Hiroshima, and, in addition, calls in as an authority on the effects of nuclear blasts a scientist or military analyst, then do the following. If the military analyst or scientist is an expert on the consequences of the disaster following a nuclear blast and at the same time is in favor of stockpiling nuclear weapons, then you should obtain this admission quickly. If the very expert employed by your opponent does not share his ultimate conclusion, then you have really embarrassed the opposition.

Second, if the alleged expert belongs to a group or espouses a cause to which you know the audience is opposed or hostile, then undermine the authority by the use of guilt by association. Surely, anyone belonging to questionable organizations is not a trustworthy authority. For example, if a policeman is accused of shooting an unarmed black man and a ballistics expert is called in to testify that the bullet was fired from that policeman's revolver, then check to see what groups the ballistics expert belongs to. If, for example, he contributes regularly to the NAACP and you are dealing with a racist audience or jury, then invoke this information in order to cast doubt on the honesty of the analysis done by the expert.

Third, an expert may be undermined by pointing out the distinction between theory and practice. Lots of things sound great in theory, such as how the computer is here to save us, and then are complete flops in practice. For example, in trying to obtain public support for a space program many experts were called upon to tell of the benefits of the research that goes on in such a program. Some of these benefits have not actually taken place. Many were based upon theoretical presuppositions that could easily be attacked. Moreover, in dealing with human problems, we are usually flooded with imbecilic theories about their solutions and we all know how many of these proposed solutions have failed. Moreover, we all know that the experts produced by our opponent are people who live in ivory towers (i.e., they teach at colleges or universities) far removed from reality.

Fourth, any authority who deals with extreme abstractions can be undermined by stressing the distinction between theory and fact. The public is frequently unaware of this distinction since the press indiscriminately reports all scientific statements as if they were facts. Many of them are purely theoretical. For example, can anyone, no matter how intelligent, really explain the beginning of the universe? If there were a beginning, then something must have preceded it. All theories rely upon some pre-existing event or thing or state like an expanding gas. This is not literally a beginning of the universe if something was already there. Besides, could we ever check such an event? Moreover, the history of science abounds with great scientists who believed false if not idiotic things. Galileo, for example, wanted to explain tides in terms of the sun. This is a little difficult to work out especially with tides at night! Kepler, despite his genius, had a whole collection of bizarre beliefs about number mysticism. Many men have made their reputations by proposing theories that were later discarded.

Fifth, as a last ditch tactic against any expert, you should engage in a general attack on all expertise. Here you can discount or dismiss an expert's knowledge by appealing to a more general truth. Suppose you are dealing with an alleged medical expert whose testimony is not to your liking. You may point out that knowledge in general is highly uncertain. And if knowledge in general is uncertain, then surely some particular kind of alleged knowledge, even medical knowledge, is uncertain. Finally, you might even hint at the fact that there is a conspiracy among all of your opponent's experts, especially if they agree.

The other general form of attack against expertise and authority is to provide counter-experts. There are two possibilities here as well. First, if you feel that you have been successful in undermining the audience's confidence in your opponent's experts, then introduce your own experts who will support your case. Second, if you had to use the fifth method outlined above—a general critique of all authority and expertise—then introduce counter-experts not necessarily as supports for your case, but simply for effect. Surely if all of these experts disagree, what is the use of using experts at all! Ridicule is the final weapon here. For example, I suggest that you consult any discussion among experts on how to raise children. One might do well to recall here William F. Buckley's quip about professors when he said that he would rather be governed by the first 100 names in the Boston telephone directory than the faculty of Harvard University.

Refutation of *Ad Populum*

Ad populum appeals by their very nature are very popular. The major ploy against them is to invoke another *ad populum* that supports your case and/or goes against the case of your opponent, one that you think might have an even greater appeal. For example, in redistricting or in choosing candidates it is frequently suggested that minority groups be placed into a stronghold or given a candidate with the same cultural background in order to guarantee them some kind of representation. This seems to be consistent with a democratic attempt to do justice to all legitimate interest groups within the society, and is thus an *ad populum* appeal. To counter it you might point out that such a system gives the minority a voice but little power, since any one representative may be ignored. In the tenth Federalist paper, James Madison argued for another ideal that is also part of the American political system of ideals, namely, the notion that a political representative should be encouraged by redistricting and other means to represent a wide variety of interests. In fact, by having a representative for a specific interest group we are encouraging factionalism, which is just the evil we want to avoid. Here we have attempted to undermine one *ad populum* appeal with another believed to have a greater appeal.

There is a second way of attacking your opponent's use of the *ad populum* appeal. This way is to be used only if you cannot think of an effective counter *ad populum* appeal. What you must then do is engage in a general attack on *ad populum* appeals. You must point out to your audience the extent to which what most people accept is wrong. You can drive this point home by giving examples, such as the fact that many people once believed that the earth was flat, and surely the majority opinion here was wrong. In the realm of values, which is more appropriate to the *ad populum* appeal, we may note that the charging of interest (usury) was once frowned upon, whereas today a vibrant economy is impossible without a credit system that depends upon charging interest.

A variation of the foregoing theme is to appeal to a value that is at once at odds with the general *ad populum* position but nevertheless shared by the narrow interests of your audience. For instance, although democracy or majority rule is part of our general *ad populum* repertory, when dealing with intellectuals in general and academics in particular you may appeal to élitism, the belief that only superior people (presumably those attached to higher education) should be allowed to make major decisions. Here derision of what the masses believe in is most appropriate and persuasive.

Refutation of Precedent

The obvious refutation of an appeal to precedent is to invoke a counterprecedent. For example, in the Supreme Court case of *Keswick v. Buick* (1937), we discover that Mr. Keswick was injured and disabled by an accident he suffered because of his recently purchased Buick automobile. It was later substantiated that the Buick was defective. Mr. Keswick sued. In its defense, the Buick lawyers argued that they should not be held responsible for the defective Buick on the grounds that such liability would economically undermine Buick in particular and the whole economy in general. Here the precedent is the security of the free enterprise system. Mr. Keswick's lawyers argued that his disability prevented him from earning a living and thereby from supporting his family. Here the counterprecedent is the preservation of the institution of the family. Mr. Keswick won.

The second way of attacking a precedent is to show that it does not apply to the case at hand because of the presence of extenuating circumstances or significant differences. Let us imagine a shipwreck and the survivors on a lifeboat far off the beaten path. Further, there are too many survivors for the small lifeboat and, in addition, there is a storm coming up. In order for some to survive, the occupants of the lifeboat must row some 1,500 miles to the nearest land. By precedent the captain should try to save everybody and in order of preference women and children should be saved first. The captain violated the precedent, first by not allowing everyone into the lifeboat, thereby causing some to perish by drowning, and second by excluding everyone other than able-bodied men and women. He was tried for murder and dereliction of duty. His defense was that precedent did not apply to his case because of extenuating circumstances. If he had followed precedent, all of them would have perished. Doing what he did, at least some were able to survive.

The third way of criticizing a precedent is to show what happens when a precedent is extended to its extreme. For example, democratic procedure is a fine precedent but inappropriate in some cases. Imagine if we had elections to determine who should purify the city water supply or how it should be purified. This should be a matter of expertise and chemistry, not democracy.

Refutation of Statistics

To begin with, one may attack the particular statistical evidence offered by an opponent in the presentation of his case. That evidence or information may simply be false. On the other hand, it may be true information but incorrectly interpreted.

How does one correctly interpret statistical evidence? To begin with, we use statistical evidence only when we cannot get at something directly. For example, I cannot directly examine tomorrow's weather, but I can present statistical evidence for what I think it might be. What I want to know about may be an individual object, person, event (tomorrow's weather), or it may be about a whole collection of things (all the swans in the world). The group of things being examined is called the *population* and the portion that I directly examine is called the sample. When we draw a conclusion about the population based upon the sample, we are making a statistical inference. If the inference is to be of any help, then the sample must not be biased or loaded. Another way of putting it is that the sample must be *random* in the sense that it represents a cross section of the whole population.

The most devastating blow that can be delivered against statistical evidence is the claim that it is not a random sample, i.e., that the sample is biased or unrepresentative. The most famous example of this is the *Literary Digest* presidential poll of 1936. We have all come to accept the general reliability of computers, which, on the basis of one percent of the vote in Oshkosh, can predict a whole national election. However, this was not always the case, especially in less sophisticated days. By polling people who were selected from a telephone directory and then calling them, the pollsters for the *Literary Digest* predicted that Alfred Landon would defeat Franklin Roosevelt handily. The sample consisted of over two million telephone calls. As we know, Roosevelt overwhelmed Landon 523 to 8 electoral votes. The sample, although large, was biased because it relied upon people who could afford a telephone during the Depression. Many of Roosevelt's supporters did not own telephones.

The trick to use here is to declare, no matter what, that your opponent's statistics are not based upon a random sample. Find a factor, any factor, and claim that the factor is crucial and has been overlooked. Here a little ingenuity will be required on your part. Keep searching until you find some factor that has been overlooked, regardless of whether it is really important, and keep harping on it. Some examples follow:

Is the sample representative in *time*? (You can always say that last year's statistics are out of date.)

Is the sample representative in *space*? (Did you interview people on the first floor, the second floor, basements, and so forth? This may seem irrelevant, but who is to say for sure?)

Is the sample representative *economically*?

Is the sample representative *geographically*? (People in the Bible Belt? People in Eastern urban areas?)

Is the sample representative by *sex*? By *marital status*? By *race*?

Is the sample representative by *age*?

In short, there are an infinite number of possibilities that might be relevant and, therefore, might be exploited. Needless to add, if you are aware of some factor that has been ignored and to which you know your audience is sympathetic, then pounce on that one.

The same technique of emphasizing a missing crucial factor may be used in attacking any graphs or charts used. Supplying the missing factor or factors, if possible, may enable you either to undermine the graphs presented or to present contrary graphs. We shall see more of this shortly.

The second way of attacking your opponent's statistics is to present a different set of statistics, one that controverts the original set. At the very least, this has the effect of neutralizing any advantage he may have gained from his initial presentation; if you have successfully challenged his statistics in a manner outlined above, then your counterstatistical evidence will prevail. For example, in order to counter one poll you may present evidence of your own poll that supports your contention. Rival political candidates frequently sponsor private polls in order to persuade potential supporters and voters that they, the candidates, are really out in front and therefore potential winners.

An especially important kind of counterstatistic is not one that contradicts the original set (your poll shows Smith is leading, your opponent's poll shows that Jones is leading), but one that supplements the original set in such a way that a different conclusion must be drawn. For example, owners of businesses (management) may point out that wages have risen at a high rate among their employees. This may very well be true. At the same time, you may present counterstatistics showing that the cost of living has risen at a staggering rate. Hence the real purchasing power of the employees' wages may be much less than at the lower wage. This kind of counterstatistic is very effective in combatting an illicit or misleading comparison. When the opposition has used a graph to present its misleading comparison, a countergraph incorporating the new statistic should be used.

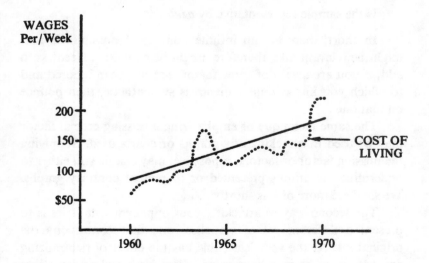

In the above graph, we assume that the opposition (employers) presented the original solid line graph, and we (the union) have superimposed the dotted line of the cost of living to show the "true" state of things.

When presenting counterstatistics you may be able to supplement them by an *ad hominem* argument as well. For example, if your opponent did not know about the existence of the counterstatistics, then you may imply that he is a fool who has not carefully researched his case. This tends to undermine the confidence of the audience in the rest of his argument as well. If your opponent is aware of the counterstatistics and he did not mention them, then you may imply that he is a scoundrel (or worse, a liar) who is deceiving the audience by suppressing relevant information. Since nobody can present every piece of information, you can always use this technique. If you are sure that the audience is with you, keep asking as a rhetorical question, "Why wasn't this information mentioned?"

If you cannot find a flaw in your opponent's statistics and if you cannot present counterstatistics, then you must engage in a general attack on the use of statistics itself. You can do this by first mentioning to your audience that every sophisticated person knows that statistical information may be misused. This is true. You then proceed to exemplify some cases of how statistics are misused.

To begin with, statistical information is information about a class of people, items, events, things, or the like. It is not really information about any individual person, item, event, or thing. Hence it is always possible that what is true of the group is not necessarily true of any individual member of that group. To say that the average American family has 2.5 children is not to say that the Smith family next door has 2.5 children. Such a state of affairs, anyway, is literally impossible. The fact that drivers under twenty-five are, statistically speaking, a greater insurance risk does not mean that every driver under twenty-five is reckless.

If your opponent has presented statistical evidence about an individual, you can always construct some evidence to prove the opposite. For example, suppose your opponent is trying to prove that Smith is a criminal type and offers the following statistical argument:

Seventy-five percent of slum dwellers are criminal types.
Smith is a slum dweller.

Therefore, it is highly probable that Smith is a criminal type.

To counter this argument and to show how ridiculous it is to use statistics, you present the following statistical argument:

> One percent of all Jehovah's Witnesses are criminal types.
> *Smith is a Jehovah's Witness.*
> _____
> Therefore, it is highly improbable that Smith is a criminal
>   type.

Your second example should be used to show that any attempt to draw conclusions from statistical evidence about the future, a process known as *extrapolation,* is risky if not impossible. Such extrapolation must be based upon the assumption that there will be no changes in circumstances and that the process being described statistically has no implications for itself. To predict the cost of living five years hence is silly without taking into account what reaction the President or the Federal Reserve Board might have if the cost of living should rise or fall drastically. Perhaps the best example of how silly extrapolation is comes from Mark Twain, who wrote the following in *Life on the Mississippi:*

> In the space of 176 years the Lower Mississippi has shortened itself 242 miles. This is an average of a trifle over one mile and a third per year. Therefore, any calm person, who is not blind or idiotic, can see that in the Old Oolithic Silurian period, just a million years ago next November, the Lower Mississippi River was upwards of one million three hundred thousand miles long, and stuck out over the Gulf of Mexico like a fishing rod. And by the same token any person can see that 742 years from now the Lower Mississippi will be only a mile and three quarters long, and Cairo and New Orleans will have joined their streets together, and be plodding comfortably along under a single mayor and a mutual board of aldermen. There is something fascinating about science. One gets such wholesome returns of conjecture out of such a trifling investment of fact.

The third example of the futility of statistics is traditionally known as the *gambler's fallacy.* As we all know, the flipping of a normal coin leads either to a head up or to a tail coming up. These are the only two possibilities. Thus there is a probability of one in two that heads will turn up. The result is called a chance event. Of course, in two flips the chance of a head turning up twice is one in four, and so on. Suppose a gambler is betting on either heads or tails and suppose further that heads has turned up five times in a row. Since he has misunderstood the probability theory the gambler may think that the probability of tails coming up after the run of heads is very great, certainly greater than one in two. He bets on tails and loses. The fallacy is in believing that the run of a chance event (heads five times in a row) alters the probability of that event (heads) in the future. Each flip of the coin is an independent event uninfluenced by past occurrences. With each flip the probability remains the same: one in two. This brings me to the final refutation of using statistics at all. Why should we believe that the chance of heads or tails is one in two? Did you ever try flipping a coin to see what happens? Try it ten times and see. (Here you might perform it for your audience and hope to get a six and four or a seven and three combination of heads and tails. If it does not work in ten tries, try twenty, and so on until the results are significantly uneven.)

Consider the following two cases of the use of statistics. A candidate for the state legislature attacks the incumbent on the grounds that the latter has missed participating in twenty-five percent of all the votes taken in the State legislature. Then it is concluded that the incumbent is not doing a responsible job. The evidence cited is a computer review of the 10,000 separate votes. Concerning these votes, we might want to ask such questions as (a) were they on significant issues or issues directly relevant to our constituency? and (b) did the incumbent's absence make a difference to the outcome? Many times, the outcome is known in advance so that the presence of some individuals is not crucial.

Our second case concerns the relative importance of class versus religion in determining the outcome of votes in which Nazis were candidates in Germany from 1929 onward. The stand-ard view is that the Nazis were put in office by the petty bourgeois (hence class is crucial). Richard F. Hamilton, on the other hand, has delved more deeply into the matter and cites statistical evidence to show that religion played a more crucial role. German farmers are routinely counted as members of the lower middle class, but Protestant farmers supported the Nazis whereas Catholic farmers did not.

While we are on the topic of statistical evidence we might point out some things about the use of *probability*. There is, to begin with, a long history of controversy within philosophy about how to interpret probability. Is probability an attribute of events, of statements, or of the attitude of the agent (gambler or social perspective)? All of these positions have been argued.

For our purposes it should be noted that the use of the calculus of probability employs mathematics and therefore gives the specious air of science to something that is questionable. The actual mathematics of probability is based upon situations where we know all of the possible outcomes, such as the fifty-two cards in a deck or the six sides of a die. Moreover, when we calculate the complex probabilities in terms of the value of simpler, related ones we should keep in mind that the original weighting comes from judgments made outside of mathematics. Even the use of relative frequency, which states what has happened in the past (e.g., the probability of precipitation in tomorrow's weather), can be questioned on the grounds that it is not a reliable guide to unique events (like tomorrow's weather) or that the notion of a random sample is not clear.

One example is the case of two gamblers who do not finish a poker game and decide to make a "fair" division of the pot. What is fair? Is it a fifty-fifty split? Or perhaps the person who has won the most so far gets the whole pot on the grounds that he had the greater probability of winning? You begin to see how difficult this is to decide.

Refutation of Theoretical Constructs

Most people distrust abstractions. Hence, in order to undermine the use of abstractions and theoretical constructs in the arguments of your opponent, you must first point out that such abstractions exist. For example, if your opponent analyzes the behavior or motivation of someone in terms of the Freudian unconscious or subconscious, you must point out that these are abstract terms. Second, no abstract term, by definition, can refer to one or more things that are directly observable. This is where audience distrust is to be exploited. Point out how impossible it is to identify the unconscious, thereby giving the impression that the thing really does not exist. For example, where would one find the unconscious or the subconscious? Under the left armpit? In the little finger? In the brain?

Refutation of Classification

In giving a critique of someone else's classification you are doing so for the benefit of the audience. Hence it is important to keep in mind the audience's point of view. The first way of undermining a classification is to find an exception. Exceptions are of two kinds: either something that does not fit at all, or something that fits in more than one place. For example, suppose someone argues that there have been no great American poets in the twentieth century. You offer as a counterexample T. S. Eliot. Your opponent replies that Eliot was a British citizen. Here you must rely upon your audience. If the audience considers Eliot an American you should press the point that the classification of great poets must include Eliot and hence your opponent's classification of great poets fails to account for something.

Eliot can serve as an example of the second kind of problem. Suppose someone is classifying poets by nationality. Is Eliot to be classified as American or as British? He was born an American but later became a British subject. W. H. Auden was born British and is now an American citizen. He might easily fit both categories and hence foul up the classification again.

Refutation of Definition

If your opponent offers a nonstandard definition, then there are two things you can do. First you should point out that the definition he used is nonstandard. If your audience is annoyed by non-standard definitions, then engage in a supplementary *ad hominem* at once. Either he is a fool who does not know what words mean, or he is a scoundrel trying to put one over on everybody.

If mere exposure does not work, then try a second kind of attack. Usually an odd definition is an attempt to make something true by definition. If this is so, then expose your opponent as offering a *circular argument* or *petito principii*. Suppose your opponent is trying to prove the existence of God and offers the following argument:

> The Bible is the word of God.
> *The Bible says that God exists.*
> Therefore, God exists.

The evidence for the existence of God is a set of statements in the Bible. When questioned as to why we should believe the Bible, our opponent argues that (1) God, by definition, is truthful, and (2) the Bible is, by definition, the word of God. Now, even if I accept the first definition there is no reason for accepting the second one. If I did not already believe in God, I would hardly accept as evidence the definition that the Bible is the word of God. The argument is circular in that it assumes what it is trying to prove. We also say that the argument is question begging since it begs (assumes) the very thing it is trying to prove. The whole controversy thus hinges upon the definition.

Consider the following definition of "democracy" supplied to us by Daniel Ortega Saavedia, the Sandinista President of Nicaragua: "Democracy is literacy, democracy is land reform, democracy is education and public health." One could ask if democracy also means majority rule, opposition candidates in elections, and a free press.

Refutation of Analogies

As we noted before, there are two kinds of analogies, literal and figurative. In the case of literal analogies one argues that similarities in several crucial respects implies similiarity in some one other respect. Since all analogies can only be partial, the refutation of a literal analogy depends upon finding one or more features that differ between the two things being compared and to press the point that it is this difference or these differences that become crucial.

The *design argument* for the existence of God is an argument from analogy. The argument says that there is an analogy between the human creation of artifacts and the Divine creation of the universe.

There are two ways of attacking an analogy. Show your opponent either that there are grave dissimilarities or that there are weaknesses in the similarities. It is more difficult to do the latter. David Hume, in fact, takes the more difficult task. What Hume argues is that there are weaknesses in both the number of common features and in the scale. Order, according to Hume, does not necessarily presuppose the existence of an agent. In the case of natural order such as in the reproduction of trees, the tree has no control over the process and merely transmits order. In the case of something done by man, man consciously employs natural processes form the outside. If a natural process exhibited anything like agent imposed order, we would be more likely to consider it a miracle rather than an example of order. Moreover, if we take the analogy seriously then the existence of evil in the world would force us to conclude that God is not all powerful. The more we make God like a human agent the more we run the danger of falling into anthropomorphism. In his *Dialogues Concerning Natural Religion* Hume writes:

> But were this world ever so perfect a production, it must still remain uncertain, whether all of the excellences of the work [world] can justly be ascribed to the workman [God]. If we survey a ship, what an exalted idea must we form of the ingenuity of the carpenter, who framed so complicated, useful, and beautiful a machine? And what surprise must we entertain, when we find him a stupid mechanic, who imitated others, and copied an art, which, through a long succession of ages, after multiplied trials, mistakes, corrections, delib-

erations, and controversies, had been gradually improving? Many worlds might have been botched and bungled, throughout an eternity, ere this system was struck out: Much labor lost: Many fruitless trials made: And a slow, but continued improvement carried on during infinite ages in the art of world-making. In such subjects, who can determine, where the truth; nay, who can conjecture where the probability, lies; amidst a great number of hypotheses which may be proposed, and a still greater number which may be imagined?

And what shadow of an argument . . . can you produce, from your hypothesis, to prove the unity of the Deity? A great number of men join in building a house or a ship, in rearing a city, in framing a commonwealth: Why may not several Deities combine in contriving and framing a world? This is only so much greater similiarity to human affairs. By sharing the work among several, we may so much farther limit the attributes of each, and get rid of that extensive power and knowledge, which must be supposed in one Deity, and which, according to you, can only serve to weaken the proof of his existence. And if such foolish, such vicious creatures as man can yet often unite in framing and executing one plan; how much more those Deities or Daemons, whom we may suppose several degrees more perfect?

. . . men are mortal, and renew their species by generation. . . . Why must this circumstance, so universal, so essential, be excluded from those numerous and limited Deities?

And why not become a perfect anthropomorphite? Why not assert the Deity or deities to be corporeal, and to have eyes, a nose, a mouth, ears, etc.?

In a word . . . a man, who follows your hypothesis, is able, perhaps, to assert, or conjecture, that the universe, sometime, arose from something like a design: But beyond that position he cannot ascertain one single circumstance. . . . This world, for aught he knows . . . was only the first rude essay of some infant Deity, who afterwards abandoned it, ashamed of his lame performance; it is the work only of some dependent, inferior Deity; and is the object of derision to his superiors: it is the production of old age and dotage in

> some superannuated Deity, and ever since his death, has run
> on at adventures. . . .

ATTACKING THE CONCLUSION

So far we have concentrated on offsetting your opponent's attempt to provide a favorable audience reaction and we have attempted specific refutations of the building blocks he needed to arrive at his conclusion. It is now time to examine the conclusion.

Before actually demolishing the conclusion you should try to make your audience realize that you have exposed cracks in the brittle structure offered by your opponent. So you should begin by offering a general characterization of your opponent's argument.

Summarize what you take to be the case of your opponent, but in order to clarify the case for the audience you should engage in a little translation so as to put that case in as bad a light as possible. Take the words used by your opponent and try to substitute those having a negative connotation in the mind of the audience. Below are a few examples of such translation.

discriminate	=	prejudice
alteration	=	radical innovation
existing order	=	antiquated prejudice
religious zeal	=	fanaticism
law and order	=	political repression

In addition, you should be as picayune as possible by picking on his actual words rather than his meaning. This task will be made especially easy for you if your opponent takes the trouble of trying to make his presentation a little stylized or literary. For example, if he talks about the economy and mentions the mysteries of the stock market, you should pick him up on his word "mystery" and declare that you are not interested in mysteries or detective stories, thereby implying that he does not know what he is talking about.

Finally, in offering a general characterization of someone else's argument, you should dismiss it or categorize it emotively in terms of some generally known position that is rejected by your audience. Thus with some audiences an entire position might be dismissed as Maxist malarky, outmoded idealism, old-fashioned liberalism, racist, or irrelevant.

After a general characterization of the argument, you should attack the route taken by your opponent to his conclusion. Here you are criticizing the means he used to go from the evidence to the conclusion. Whether or not he is guilty of them, you can accuse him of certain traditional formal fallacies. Moreover, where possible, you should use the *Latin names* of these fallacies because this will make the audience believe you are skilled in identifying such fallacies and because the error sounds so much worse, just like a rare disease, when described in Latin.

> *Argumentum ad Baculum* (appeal to force)
> *Argumentum ad Hominem* (attack the man/person)
> *Argumentum ad Ignorantiam* (argument from ignorance)
> *Argumentum ad Misericordiam* (appeal to pity)
> *Argumentum ad Populum* (appeal to the people)
> *Argumentum ad Verecundiam* (appeal to authority)
> *Petito Principii* (begging the question)
> *Ignoratio Elenchi* (irrelevant conclusion)

Hasty Generalization

If your opponent has used statistical information or particular facts of any kind to arrive at a generalization, then you should claim that the generalization was too hasty. This can be done in one of two ways. Either you provide evidence of an exception to his generalization, or you argue that he did not examine enough cases even if you cannot think of a counterinstance. A variation of this argument is the claim that no adequate sample was used.

For example, suppose a census taker interviews five people in a city and discovers that the first five people he interviews are named John Smith. If he then concludes that everyone in the city must be named John Smith, then his generalization is too hasty.

Try to impress upon the audience the foolhardiness of any generalization by thinking of an example that they will recognize as too hasty. For example, if your opponent is trying to characterize Orientals as not being ready for democracy, you might point out to an audience of those who are sympathetic to the plight of black people that the same sort of argument was used by Southern racists for not granting blacks the right to vote. Southerners were a bit too hasty; maybe your opponent is too.

Composition

The fallacy of composition is another instance of an error of arguing from individual cases to a general case or to a whole. If I examine individual baboons and find that each one separately is cowardly, may I conclude that a pack of baboons will also be cowardly? The answer is no. When in a group, baboons become extremely aggressive. This principle is used by military men who know that the properties of parts (individual soldiers) are not necessarily the properties of the whole (an army). It also finds application among rabble-rousers and organizers of demonstrations. People who are otherwise rational become overly emotional and irrational when formed into a group. Or should I say mob?

The difference between composition and hasty generalization is that in hasty generalization I am making a prediction about the next individual I come across based upon the examination of other individuals of the same kind. Thus, to infer that the next crow I see will be black on the basis of crows I have seen in the past might be a hasty generalization. In composition I am talking about a whole and its parts. If I have individually great architects design individually beautiful buildings, does this mean that a whole city composed of individually beautiful buildings is also beautiful? Not necessarily, because the architecture of the individual buildings may clash. It is also conceivable that a mishmash of ugliness may, on sum, turn out to be very exciting.

You may accuse your opponent of the fallacy of composition whenever he implies that a whole has (or does not have) a property because the parts have (or do not have) it. For example, your opponent may argue that an organization is undemocratic because the executive committee is appointed by different groups rather than elected. On the other hand, he fails to mention that decisions of the executive committee are by majority vote. The executive committee is democratic. It is not necessary that every part of an organization be democratic in order for the whole organization to be considered democratic.

Division

Now we are concerned with arguments that move from a general principle to a particular case. One may, of course, have already attacked the general principle. On the other hand, one may accept the general principle but argue that it is not sufficient to establish the conclusion one's opponent wishes to draw from it.

The fallacy of division is that of believing some property of a whole to be automatically a property of every part of that whole. For example, a work of art may be beautiful, but this in no way means that every part of that work of art is beautiful and therefore indispensable. Is the Venus de Milo not beautiful because the arms are missing? Another example is the great team that fails to have a single all-star on it. The quality of a whole, being a great team, is not necessarily a quality of every member. It works the other way as well in that individually great players may not be able to mesh and form a great team. Thus the fallacy of division is the opposite of the fallacy of composition.

Accident

In the fallacy of accident one mistakenly applies a general principle to a specific case without realizing that the circumstances (accidents) of the individual case make the general principle inapplicable. As an example of this, I am reminded of a scene from the movie *Dr. Strangelove* in which a mad general has ordered his planes to initiate an atomic war without instructions from the Pentagon. Another officer attempts to phone Washington from a pay phone in order to report the emergency but finds that he has no change. There is a vending machine nearby and the officer asks one of his men to break into it in order to obtain some change. The enlisted man refuses on the grounds that the vending machine is private property. No doubt one should not destroy private property (general principle), but in the case of preventing an atomic war (exception) the accidental circumstances invalidate the general principle.

When accusing someone of the fallacy of accident one could argue that what he is really saying is that one general principle takes precedence over another general principle. Thus he is accusing his opponent of not clearly seeing the real problem at hand. And, in general, this is what happens in an argument where two sides view the problem from different perspectives. All of this should reinforce how important it is to establish the best generalizations, in the sense of the most defensible ones, in the early part of your argument.

Another example of accident is the argument that some people should not be punished for committing crimes (general principle) because (accidental circumstances) they are either insane or victims of their environment. We shall be discussing this later.

Characterizing the Conclusion (Dilemma)

The only test of a conclusion or principle is to extend it to the extreme in order to see how well it works. Thus whenever your opponent gives his conclusion, assume that he means it to be a general principle. For example, if he concludes that we should send aid to a country in distress (for example, Ethiopia), then you should assume that he wants to send aid to every country in distress. If he attempts to reject this notion, then counter by asking why some are to be favored over others.

The second way of directly attacking the conclusion is to criticize it for not achieving some other function or goal. For example, if you are arguing against aiding the Ethiopians, then you should point out that such aid will in no way end the hostilities in Africa. The specific function not achieved should be something that you think the audience considers important.

The third way of attacking a conclusion directly is to treat your opponent's conclusion as contrary and not as contradictory. What does this mean? Usually, you and your opponent have contradictory positions, and when it becomes difficult to attack the contradictory statement, you may pretend that his position is something else, something you can attack more easily. Usually what you can attack more easily is the contrary statement. Let me give an example.

A. McCarthy was not a great threat.
B. McCarthy was a great threat.
C. McCarthy was no threat.

Statements A and B are contradictories. Statements B and C are contraries. A and B cannot be both true or both false at the same time. B and C can both be false at the same time but not both true.

If you are arguing B, that McCarthy was a great threat, and your opponent is arguing A, that McCarthy was not a great threat, then you should pretend that your opponent is really saying that *C,* McCarthy was no threat. In fact, I have just seen such an argument used in a review in *The New York Times Book Review.* One man attempted to minimize, but not deny, the McCarthy threat and the reviewer simply accused him of not seeing any threat. If this kind of activity is good enough for *The New York Times,* it is certainly good enough for you.

One of the best ways of concluding a refutation of someone else's argument is to offer a *dilemma.* The structure of a dilemma will be given first, then exemplified and analyzed.

If . . . S_1 . . ., then . . . S_2 . . .; *and*
If . . . S_3 . . . , then . . . S_4 . . .
S_1 or S_3.

Therefore, S_2 or S_4.

Consider the following example of a dilemma:

If men are good, then gun control laws are not necessary; *and* if men are bad, gun control laws will not be effective. Men are either good *or* bad. Therefore, gun control laws are either not necessary *or* not effective.

In the above example, S_1 corresponds to the statement "men are good." S_2 corresponds to the statement "gun control laws are not necessary." S_3 corresponds to the statement "men are bad." S_4 corresponds to the statement "gun control laws will not be effective."

The dilemma is an effective weapon because it leaves the impression that your opponent's case leads only to undesirable consequences. Since the dilemma has a standard pattern, there is no challenge in constructing it. However, it is always the case that some dilemmas are better than others. The most effective ones are built from points you have already made. Thus, in the structure you should try to argue the relationship between S_1 and S_2 or the relationship between S_3 and S_4 in the earlier part of your attack. If they seem to be successful, then you may use them in the dilemma. This technique has a way of reinforcing your whole argument in the minds of the audience. Moreover, S_1 and S_3 should be a dichotomy that you think your audience will accept.

For example, in arguing against a dual legislature, the famous French Abbé Sieyès pounded away at the fact that two legislatures wasted a great deal of time duplicating each other's effort. Later he pointed out the difficulties that would follow if the two legislatures disagreed with each other. He was then able to summarize neatly his opposition in a dilemma: If the second legislature agrees with the first legislature, then the second one is superfluous; and if the second legislature disagrees with the first legislature, then the second one is pernicious. The second legislature must either agree or disagree with the first one. Therefore, the second legislature is either superfluous or pernicious.

Nonverbal Devices

There is no reason that an attacker cannot use the same nonverbal devices as used by one who presents an argument. Therefore, you should consult the end of chapter 1 for a survey of such devices. Moreover, you will have had an opportunity to survey which of these devices, if used by your opponent, was most effective and take steps to counteract it.

In addition to the foregoing devices, you should remember

that a good attacker tries to choose the battlefield. That is, he tries to give the impression that his interpretation of the opposition is the only one as well as the correct one. This task will be easier if you can, as part of your attack, divert the audience's attention from your opponent while he is presenting his case. Perhaps the most famous single example of such a technique was used by the great trial lawyer Clarence Darrow. During the presentation of the prosecution's case Darrow began to smoke a very long cigar and did not flick off the ash. After a while everyone in the courtroom, including the jury, began to look at Darrow's cigar in anxious anticipation of the falling of the ash. The ash never fell, and the jury never really paid attention to the prosecution. The secret was a thin wire inserted in the center of the cigar so that the ash would be supported.

FACE-TO-FACE DEBATE

In addition to the techniques we have already discussed, there are some special things to keep in mind if you are engaged in a face-to-face debate, cross-examinations of your opponents, or the give and take of common discussions.

There are three aims in any face-to-face debate: first, and foremost, you are trying to elicit a contradiction from your opponent; second, you are trying to embarrass the opposition publicly; third, you are trying to convince the audience of your proficiency.

Questioning

When asking questions of your opposition your major aim is to elicit a contradiction. You do this primarily by getting him to make two contradictory statements. Since he is likely to be looking out for this possibility, it is better to *hide the conclusion* toward which you are driving. In addition, you might ask leading questions, surreptitiously introduce the premises you want brought out, and mix up the order so that it is not apparent in what direction you are going. The classic master at this sort of game is none other than Socrates. In fact, the *Socratic method* is most easily identified as the method of eliciting contradictions from an opponent. A famous example of this technique is to be found in Plato's *Republic* in a discussion of the nature of justice. The major participants in the discussion are Socrates and Thrasymachus, who argues that justice is whatever is in the interest of the stronger party (a variation of the position that "might makes right"). Socrates proceeds to question Thrasymachus to see if the position can withstand analysis.

> THRASYMACHUS: The laws are made by the ruling party in its own interest; a democracy makes democratic laws, a despot despotic ones, and so on. By making these laws they define as "right" for their subjects whatever is for their interest, and they call anyone who breaks these laws a wrongdoer and punish him accordingly. That is what I mean: in all states alike "right" has the same meaning, namely, what is in the interest of the party established in power, and that is the strongest. So the sound conclusion is that what is "right" is the same everywhere: the interest of the stronger party. . . .
>
> SOCRATES: No doubt you also think it is right to obey the men in power.
>
> THRASYMACHUS: I do.
>
> SOCRATES: Are they infallible in every type of state, or do they sometimes make mistakes?
>
> THRASYMACHUS: Of course they can make a mistake.
>
> SOCRATES: In framing laws, then, they may do their work well or badly?
>
> THRASYMACHUS: No doubt. . . .
>
> SOCRATES: But the subjects are to obey any law they lay down, and they will then be doing right?
>
> THRASYMACHUS: Of course.
>
> SOCRATES: If so by your account, it will be right to do what is not to the interest of the stronger party as well as what is.
>
> THRASYMACHUS: What's that you're saying?
>
> SOCRATES: Just what you said, I believe. . . . Haven't you admitted that the rulers . . . sometimes mistake their

> own best interests, and that at the same time it is right
> for the subjects to obey? . . .
>
> THRASYMACHUS: Yes, I suppose so.
>
> SOCRATES: Well that amounts to admitting that it is right
> to do what is not to the interest of the rulers or the
> stronger party. . . . You with your intelligence must see
> how that follows.

While a verbal admission of a contradiction is the most effective way of refuting an opponent, it is not always possible to obtain one. The next best thing is to point out, if possible, a contradiction or inconsistency between the spoken word and behavior. For instance, when someone attacks the capitalist system and praises what Socialist countries try to do, you might ask him why he doesn't live in one.

If you cannot elicit the contradiction in a formal or informal way, proceed next to try to get your opponent to become angry. Members of the audience are always ready to laugh and angering your opponent may lead him to say foolish things.

If you find that you are succeeding in your questioning and that your opponent knows this, then you may find that he refuses to accept anything you say without qualification. He may do this to stymie the progress of your line of questioning. At this point you should inject a truism like "Isn't your name . . ." or, "Isn't today's date. . . ." He must either say yes, in which case you can congratulate him on being able to answer questions and then continue with your line of argument; or he can continue to say no and embarrass himself.

Another way of obtaining an answer you want is to ask a loaded or *complex question,* a question so phrased that any answer given is incriminating. Actually, a complex question is really several questions in one. For example, if I ask "Are you still a member of the Communist party?" there are two possible answers. If the answer is no, then the person questioned has admitted his past membership in the Communist party. If the answer is yes, then the person has still admitted his past membership in the party. Either way, he has admitted membership. What should *he* do if he were clever and never a member of the Communist party? Rather than reply with yes or no, he should simply say that he has never belonged to the party.

Answering

Although this is a chapter on attacking someone else's case, since we have already introduced the topic of face-to-face debate, we should consider ways of answering or defending oneself in this kind of confrontation. This will lead naturally into the next chapter.

Just as the major objective of the person asking the questions is to expose a contradiction, so the major objective of the person answering the questions is to avoid a contradiction. If you discover the ultimate contradiction toward which your opponent is leading you, quickly change the subject or try to move off on a tangent and thus lead the discussion away from that issue.

If the discussion turns on some crucial matter of fact, which if answered will lead to a contradiction, then instead of denying its truth (which might prove embarrassing if you are wrong) simply declare that you are an incompetent judge on that subject and refrain from expressing an opinion. Usually it is not good form to admit ignorance, but in this case it is more important to avoid stepping into a contradiction.

One of the devices used to shake up, anger, or embarrass you will be for your opponent to declare that he does not understand what you are saying. This is usually stated in a manner indicating that you are unclear or just plain confused. Places where this device is frequently used are in the classroom where teachers use it against students and at academic gatherings where senior colleagues use it against junior colleagues. When confronted by the charge of a lack of clarity you should reply along the following lines:

"Please excuse me [ironic politeness], but with your great intellect, it should be easy to understand anything. It must be my poor judgment of the issue."

Follow this by a really simple statement of the issue, that is, explain it in a patronizing manner as if the questioner were a moron. If he persists in declaring your presentation unclear, then conclude by saying, "Some people see and some people do not."

Six

Defending Your Case

Among sophists there is an age-old debate about how much of a defense should be included in an initial presentation. Some feel that you should automatically defend your case by negating possible objections in the minds of the audience before they are even presented so as to leave no room for the opposition to maneuver. One objection to combining a defense along with a presentation is that the presentation tends to become obscured when lumped with a defense, a defense that inevitably includes an attack on the alternatives. Moreover, it tends to make you look defensive, as if you had something that could not stand by itself. I think that it should also be clear, from a careful reading of chapter 2, that there are ways of attacking a case regardless of how it is initially presented. You cannot defuse every attacking bomb.

The purists, in addition, want to present their case unencumbered by any defense. They are proud of their ability to rebut and so welcome any and all objections, even objections by the sophisticated, because it gives them the opportunity to counterattack and object to the objectors. They can proudly point to the fact that most formal discussions allow for this sort of see-saw action. Debates usually include three parts: a presentation, a questioning period (a form of attack and defense), and an opportunity for rebuttal. The courts give both the prosecution and the defense an opportunity for an introductory statement, the presentation of a case, cross-examination, and an opportunity for a summation. There are, however, two general objections to this procedure.

First, it is not always possible to get back at your opposition. The format, the audience, or the medium may only allow a single exposure. Moreover, some people lack the quickness of wit to respond rapidly in the give and take and they wish to rely more heavily upon a well thought out presentation and defense. I might add that if you are also thinking about your defense while you are preparing your presentation, you might come up with a better presentation and a better defense because you have anticipated what the objections might be.

The moral of this debate is that you must let the circumstances determine the extent to which you combine a presentation with a defense. In any case, it is still useful to separate the different techniques of each so as to make you more self-conscious and adept at both using them and spotting them as used by others.

As is always the case when you are trying to win, the major thing to look for is audience reaction. Try to determine the extent to which your objector has been successful in breaching your defense. What particular points of yours were most easily overwhelmed, which remained steadfast and resisted all assaults, and, especially, which were ignored by the opposition? Sometimes ignoring a particular point or points is symptomatic of the opposition's inability to overcome it or the opposition's recognition that the point is so formidable it is best to call as little attention to it as possible. Your evaluation of what worked and what did not work with the audience should determine what you choose to emphasize, what you choose to ignore, and what new elements you should introduce into your defense.

There is, however, a special personal element that must be taken into account when we move to the defense, and that is your own emotional reaction to being attacked. It is one thing to be a spectator at a battle and it is quite another to be a participant. Reactions will vary with the individual, but in all cases you must learn to control your emotional responses and concentrate on winning. This suggests certain general rules for controlling yourself:

Never admit defeat:
Certainly neither look as if you have been, nor feel that you have been, defeated. If the audience detects a feeling of low morale in you, then it will immediately assume your opponent has won. There are several things you might do; for example, sit with your hands folded, avoid squirming, laugh louder than anyone else when he makes a joke, smile, take notes but not too many and take no notes at the end, or maybe pull out a copy of the *New York Review of Books* and read it, ignoring your opponent altogether if you think you can get away with it.

Refuse to be convinced:
Even if you feel that he has a good argument and that your case is weaker, refuse to be convinced of your opponent's case. This is especially important. If we give up because the opposition appears to be right we inevitably discover after it is too late that we were really right in the first place. How often have you thought of an adequate answer and rebuttal after the debate was over? Trust your initial instincts!

Retain your self-confidence:
It always hurts to have someone think ill either of you or your case, especially if your opponent has some sort of prestige. In order to build up your self-confidence and to offset the image you have of your opposition, try the following. Imagine that the man or woman who has attacked you is standing there without any clothes on. This is enough to make anybody look ridiculous. Or imagine the special kind of ignorance, stupidity, blindness, or combinations thereof that might possibly lead someone to disagree with your case.

Do not underestimate the opposition:
If you do you are likely to let your guard down and cause your opposition to win by your own default. The best way to accomplish this general end and to retain your self-confidence is to think of your opposition as *evil*. It is not just the case that the opposition is wrong, but it is also dishonest and unscrupulous in intent.

A defense is also an attack:
Do not simply defend your own position but attack the opposition as well. You attack not only to show that the argument of the opposition is merely persuasive in a superficial way, but also to give yourself more time to think of a reply in defending your own case. But at all times give the impression that you are in charge of the argument.

COUNTERATTACK

Every defense must have a counterattack, that is, a refutation of the charges made against your case by the opposition. Needless to say, not every attack against your case will contain every kind of charge, so you will have to choose from the following techniques, depending upon what your opponent uses.

Statement of Your Case

There is one thing you should always claim no matter what the opposition has said, namely, that the opposition has misstated your case. No matter what the opposition has said, you should make this claim because *(a)* if the opposition has misstated your case because it misunderstood your case, then by implication the opposition might not be very bright; *(b)* if the opposition has misstated your case but understands your case very well, then by implication the opposition is dishonest; *(c)* this gives you the opportunity to restate your case, and you want to restate your case so as (1) to reinforce in the minds of the audience what you want to discuss; (2) to reformulate your case in order to sidestep some of the objections made, a point we shall see in greater detail below; and finally (3) to give yourself a little more time before you reply.

All or Nothing Mistake

Since one of the major ways in which a case is attacked is to extend it to an extreme (a point we made earlier), you must be prepared to offset this kind of tactic if it is used against you. If you did not make a generalization or categorical statement and your opponent accuses you of having done so, then reiterate the more modest case you were presenting. In addition imply that your opponent is so intent upon seeing every issue as clearly black and white that he misses all of the subtleties and nuances of your argument. For example, in arguing for the use of quotas in affirmative action, you admit all the shortcomings of the program, but you reiterate that it is temporary and superior to any other program that has been tried. It is not a panacea, but it does do some good. Moreover, reiterate that you are not opposed to other programs.

As another example, suppose you argue that nationalism or national pride was a major if not the major factor in the colonization of Africa and Asia by Western European countries during the nineteenth and early twentieth centuries. Your opponent might counter with the Marxist-Leninist thesis of imperialism by pointing out the economic advantages that colonial powers expected or obtained. Not only are there exceptions to your opponent's case (you show he is wrong), but you do not have to deny his point in order to substantiate your own. It may very well be true that economic gain was one factor in colonization, but this does not show that nationalism was not also a factor. In fact you can still argue that nationalism was more important as a factor than economics.

Appeal to Ignorance

The inability to disprove your case is tantamount to a proof that it is correct. As long as nobody can show that you are absolutely mistaken, then act as if you are absolutely right. Keep harping upon the fact that some of the things you said, even if they are trivial, are right and that the opposition cannot disprove your case.

There are two good examples of this. First, how would someone go about disproving the existence of God? In the case of something like God, I do not see how one can.

Second, no conspiracy theory can be disproved. How would one go about showing that all of the conspiracy explanations of how President John F. Kennedy was killed are incorrect? As long as the conspiracy theories are *compatible* with the known evidence, no disproof is possible. Of course compatibility is not the same thing as proof for the simple reason that an infinite number of compatible possibilities can be invented. Nevertheless, there is in the popular mind the irresistible temptation to take compatibility for proof.

Statistics

If you used statistics, and if your opponent attacked your use of statistics in the manner we indicated in chapter 5, then your defense should be as follows. On the one hand, if he accuses you of not using a random, representative, or adequate sample, you counter this by asking him to *define what a random sample is.* He will be unable to define a random sample because no one, not even the most sophisticated statistical analyst, has been able to define a random sample. The reason for this is interesting and worth dwelling upon.

Statistical information consists of a mathematically expressed relationship between two or more things. For example, the number of smallpox cases decreases in an area or within a group when those people are inoculated. Perhaps there is an 88 percent decrease in the number of cases. However, no amount of statistical information can establish an invariable or causal relationship between two more things without independent evidence. The whole point of using statistical evidence is that it is only used *when we do not know the direct connection* or complex of connections among things.

For example, in studying crime statistics we may note a high correlation between crime and membership in certain ethnic groups. What does this tell us? That members of certain groups are more criminally prone? That there is a police conspiracy to arrest or pursue more vigorously members of certain ethnic groups? That there is a hidden cause or causes (another factor) that might lead members of a certain ethnic group to commit more crime? One may use statistical evidence to discover a problem (you notice high correlations that may or may not mean anything) or to back up some theory about why certain things happen. But without the theory, the evidence makes no sense. Hence statistical evidence by itself does not prove or disprove anything, but together with other pieces of information it may be meaningful. Anyone who attacks your statistical evidence and ignores the rest of your case can have this truth pointed out to him and to the audience.

On the other hand, if your opponent attacks the use of statistics in general, you may provide a counterexample to show how silly that would be. Suppose there were a dread disease that did not exist among a certain portion of the population because they ate a certain food. In other words, a high statistical correlation exists between a food and the absence of a disease. Wouldn't you eat that food even though the direct connection is unknown to you?

As for the charge that you either neglected or suppressed certain facts, you may make the same countercharge by introducing some facts that you had not mentioned before and turning the question on your adversary. Why didn't he mention that information? This, by the way, reinforces an earlier point we made about saving some ammunition for later instead of using everything in your initial presentation.

Defense of Generalizations

Your generalizations are attacked when someone tries to point out that there is an exception to them. There are three answers to this charge.

First, the exception may be irrelevant to the point you are trying to make. For example, suppose you have tried to argue that there is a connection between rock music and the drug culture, and as part of your evidence you cite cases of rock stars like Boy George who are involved with drugs. You may even indicate how the lyrics of some songs and the use of drugs during performances by both performers and members of the audience is part of the scene. Your opponent may point out that some rock stars are not involved in the drug culture. What your opponent says is true but perhaps still irrelevant to your generalization or to your contention that there is some kind of deep connection. To be sure, star athletes have been found to be drug users but no one claims that sports is part of the drug culture. However, the use of drugs is not part of the normal audience reaction at say a basketball game, and the values articulated in professional sports do not dwell on the pleasures of drug taking.

Second, you may claim that the exception is not really an exception and accuse your opponent of *special pleading*. You argue that the grounds on which he claims to make an exception (attacks based on the charges of accident or division) are not good grounds. For example, during the 1970 trial of Black Panther leader Bobby Seale, William Sloan Coffin, chaplain at Yale University, argued that Seale should not be tried, convicted, and punished even if he were guilty, because society had been responsible for making him a criminal. This is an exception by genetic explanation. You might argue that this is special pleading. Would Coffin want to release a Southern rascist who led a lynch mob on the grounds that society (in the form of Reconstruction) had caused this man to become a kind of criminal? To argue for the genetic explanation in one case and not in the other is to be guilty of special pleading.

The third defense against the charge of a hasty generalization (or the existence of an exception to your generalization) is to fall back on the wise saying that "the exception proves the rule" and hope for the best. This, by the way, implies (but don't tell anyone about it) that the more exceptions there are the better the rule is. That does sound strange! Actually, the original statement was made by Francis Bacon and when he said it the word "prove" meant "test." You test a generalization by looking for exceptions. Rather than helping the generalization, the exception invalidates it.

In Defense of Definitions

Defenses can be challenged as being either too strict or too permissive in the sense of being unusual. If you are charged with taking terms too narrowly, and especially if you are charged with making your position true by definition, then reply that we must have clear thoughts, otherwise equivocation will be the undoing of us all. Enter into a tirade about how your opponent is a sloppy thinker who objects to those who strive for clarity.

Suppose you are charged with misusing a word, misusing it in the sense that your use is not recognized by the dictionary. What do you do? Here you enter into a tirade against dictionaries. By whom and how are dictionaries put together? What makes these men qualified to decide?

The question is, are dictionaries descriptive or normative? That is, do they describe actual usage or do they prescribe how we ought to use a term? If they are descriptive, then the dictionary is obviously incorrect because it does not describe how you use the term. If it is replied that dictionaries describe general usage and not peculiar usage, then cast doubt on this. Have you ever been polled by a dictionary maker on how you use a term? Has there ever been a national referendum on usage?

Now try the other approach. Suppose dictionaries are prescriptive, that is, they tell us how we ought to use a word. Who are the dictionary makers to decide such crucial issues in life anyway? Are they people who already hold views opposed to yours? If so, then it is the dictionary makers who are trying to win arguments by making certain views true by definition. Moreover, if this keeps up we shall end up with what Orwell described in *1984* as Newspeak, a language constantly manipulated for the benefit of a few.

Even when we deal with nominal definitions (true by human convention) we can have reasons for selecting one definition rather than another. Arguments in favor of your definition may be (a) etymological (citing the origin of the word), (b) conditions for its use, or (c) consequences of using it.

Consider, for example, the charge that what you have said is tautological, i.e., true by definition. Let us suppose that what you have said is that increasing the money supply (which diminishes the value of money because there is now more of it) brings about an increase in prices (inflation). In an obvious sense this is not a cause and effect relationship but a matter of definition. However, this definition in conjunction with some economic theories can provide all kinds of useful predictions. By themselves, definitions mean little, but in tandem with other things they can be highly significant. It is therefore not just the definition that is at issue but the other elements you employ with it.

Quoting Out of Context

Like any other charge, this one should be denied and continually denied. Keep insisting that the words you quoted are exactly as you said they were, that is, you ignore the charge that you quoted out of context and pretend that you were charged with misquoting.

If your opponent pursues this point or if you are forced to engage in a prolonged discussion of it, then raise the broader issue of what constitutes the proper context. Is it the phrase, sentence, or sentences you quoted, or is it something larger? Accuse your opponent of being ornery: If I quote the sentence, then he will say I did not quote the whole paragraph, and if I quote the whole paragraph then he will say that I deliberately ignored the preceding or following paragraphs, until finally I shall have to end up quoting everything written in the English language—or is that too small a context?

If you are really trapped by a skillful adversary who finds some way of convincing the audience that you have used an improper or misleading linguistic context, then claim that the proper context includes the gestures and behavior of the person you quoted. Since there is no generally agreed upon context in terms of which we interpret gestures and behavior, who can really accuse one of misreading someone else's position?

Legal minds, particularly those of scholars of the U.S. Constitution, have a flair for this kind of interpretation. Some of them are said to be "loose constructionists" of the Constitution, and others are said to be "strict constructionists." Much is made of this distinction, but actually there is little to be said for it. If anyone were really strict he could never extend or apply the Constitution to a single case. Every reading involves an interpretation. When we speak of the spirit of the law, we are advocating a much freer interpretation. But what exactly did the framers of the Constitution mean by some of the things they said? For an understanding of this, we have to consult some of their other writings, and this is exactly what is done. But which other writings? What is the proper context? This is a real problem even when we are not trying to be devious.

Inconsistency

If you are accused of being inconsistent, deny it! Deny it! First, there may be a simple misunderstanding involved and you can easily clear it up. Second, there may be no problem at all and the accusation is merely an attempt on the part of the opposition to embarrass you. In this case, you should point it out and publicly chastise the opposition. Third, there may very well be an overlooked inconsistency. In this case, you should confidently move to reinterpret what you said so as to make the contradiction disappear.

For example, suppose you are advocating social reform for an oppressed group of people and you publicly argue that the oppressed must take the law into their own hands, they must use violence to get justice; you then pull out a machete and wave it while you quote Patrick Henry's famous statement, "Give me liberty or give me death!" Later, when you are arrested and tried for inciting to riot, sedition, or some similar charge, you claim that you made no such inflammatory remarks, because your words were not to be taken literally, they were only political rhetoric. What you had really meant was that people should only do this if necessary or forced to but actually at this time you really believe that conditions will allow for more moderate means of social reform.

Depending upon the situation and the audience, there may be times when inconsistency is not a bad thing. After all, is not a foolish consistency the hobgoblin of little minds? All right, then, I am inconsistent. So what of it?

This technique is especially useful when you invoke a higher truth than the limited ones to which the laws of inconsistency apply. In a more serious vein, we note that there is a difference between incompatibility and contradiction. In the case of a contradiction both statements cannot be true at the same time. In the case of incompatibility, or the charge by your opponent that you are making incompatible statements, the incompatibility exists only relevant to some particular framework, which one need not accept. For example, the United States is a democracy in which the majority rules. Yet in order to amend the Constitution we need the approval of two-thirds of the states, which is more than a majority and not linked to actual population. A minority of slightly more than one-third of the states can block a change. Is this not a contradiction? Is it incompatibility? The rebuttal to these charges is that normally the majority rules, but in case of major changes we need a very large majority in order to insure stability and be consistent with the original agreement. After all, two-thirds of the states could vote to repeal the two-thirds rule!

Red Herring

So far we have been discussing refutations of specific charges made against your presentation. If you have successfuly rebutted them, all well and good. But what happens if you feel that your defense has not been strong enough or that there are lingering doubts in the minds of the audience? At this point you should avoid sticking to the point. Remember that the only thing that always sticks to the point is a dead insect on display. What you must do is draw attention to a side issue where you feel particularly strong. This will give the impression that you are still in charge of the course of the discussion.

There are several things to keep in mind when casting out a red herring. First, although it is a side issue, it must be related at least indirectly to the issue you are discussing, otherwise the audience will not accept it. When discussing astronomy, one cannot introduce as a red herring the question about the price of eggs.

Second, the issue you introduce must have sufficient emotional appeal to catch attention immediately. It should be so strong that you can work it as long as you want. Third, you must make sure that you present this issue in such a way that you and the audience inevitably end up on the same side while your opponent ends up on the other side.

A particularly interesting version of the red herring is to be found in the discussions concerning cures for social ills. Imagine a debate about improving the education of ghetto children wherein Side One claims that some proposal (let us call it X) is the way to solve the problem. Let us suppose further that Side Two attacks X on the grounds that it is inherently self-contradictory, has failed when used before, will interfere with other programs, and costs too much anyway. Side One, in defense of its proposal, introduces the following red herring: you do not really understand and sympathize with the problem. Side One then proceeds to elaborate a lengthy presentation of the problem: the horror of the ghetto, the warped lives of the children, the lack of a future, and their eventual destruction. By the end of this red herring, the audience is in tears. If the audience does not think that Side Two is racist, it certainly thinks Side Two is insensitive. Moreover, the audience will not only approve of proposal X, they would probably approve of any proposal.

Why is this a red herring? The argument was about a specific proposal X to solve a particular problem. At no time was the problem itself under discussion. Side Two never denied the existence of the problem, it only attacked proposal X as a way of solving the problem. Side One, which defended proposal X, never really answered the criticisms but instead acted as if Side Two was denying the existence of the problem. The red herring was related (at least in content), it was highly emotional, and Side One took the side it believed would be shared by the audience.

Call for Perfection

One possibility should never be forgotten: your case or proposal may be a good one but it may not be perfect. That is, there may be problems or objections to it that cannot be satisfactorily answered. This, however, does not imply that your solution is not the best available. There are times when it is necessary to admit that there are objections but they do not invalidate your proposal. Here you accuse your opposition of wanting perfection or Utopia before they will accept any proposal.

This kind of problem, objection, and defense figured very prominently during the debate over civil rights legislation. Civil rights advocates had introduced legislation designed to protect blacks against race prejudice and harassment. The opponents of civil rights legislation argued that the only way the race prejudice problem would be solved (really) was when some men experienced a change of heart. Legislation would not do the trick. In answer to this objection, civil rights advocates (including Martin Luther King, Jr.) pointed out that they did not have time to wait for a perfect mankind. In the meantime the laws would at least change behavior, and that was some kind of progress even if it was not Utopia.

As a supplement to this kind of defense you can argue that your proposal will, or might eventually, lead to removing all difficulties. As Dr. King pointed out, the change in men's behavior, created by the laws, might eventually lead to changes in their hearts.

Nothing-but Objections

A variation of the call for perfection is the simple articulation of objections. The problem is not whether my proposal is perfect, but whether it would be better to do nothing or even whether there is an alternative.

There are two versions of the defense against nothing-but objections. We might call version one the "less sincere" version. Here we argue that even though our proposal is not perfect we should all adopt it anyway because no one can think of a better one. I offer the three following examples of the less sincere version. (1) Cure for cancer: periodic human sacrifice to the sun god; (2) Cure for war: drinking milk shakes; (3) Removal of warts:

drinking Irish whiskey. No doubt there are people who will not like my suggested solutions, but can they offer an alternative that will prove to be more immediately successful?

The second version should be called the "more sincere" version. There, as is so often the case in life's great moral dilemmas, we must choose between two evils and hope that we choose the lesser. It is very important in cases like this that they involve two clear and evil courses of action with no other alternatives. Imagine you are trapped in a tower with a mentally deranged man who (1) does not know you are present, and (2) is shooting at and killing people passing below. Every second you hesitate he kills another person; he is too strong for you to overpower; there is no prospect of immediate help from the outside; the only way you can stop him is to kill him from behind with the small hand gun you have. Should you kill him? No doubt this is not a pleasant decision and you will be destroying life. On the other hand, what is the alternative? Can you seriously hesitate because someone else might later object to the taking of life?

Damning the Dilemma

There are three ways of handling a dilemma, but before we discuss them let us remind ourselves what a dilemma is. A dilemma supposedly offers you two alternatively undesirable consequences. It is an argument having two premises and a conclusion:

If . . . S_1 . . . then S_2 . . .; *and if* . . . S_3 . . . then S_4.

S_1 *or* S_3.

Therefore, S_2 *or* S_4.

The following is an example of a dilemma:

If the police are given a free hand, then they will interfere with our civil liberties; *and* if the police are not given a free hand, then they will not be able to prevent crime. Either the police are given a free hand *or* they are not given a free hand. *Therefore,* the police must either interfere with our civil liberties *or* the police will not be able to suppress or prevent crime.

The first way of answering a dilemma is to *grasp one or the other horn.* We do this by rejecting the truth of one or the other conditional statements (a conditional statement is a statement of the "if . . . then" form). In our example we have two conditionals: if the police are given a free hand, then they will interfere with our civil liberties; *and* if the police are not given a free hand, then they will not be able to prevent crime.

We might easily reject the latter conditional by pointing out that the police do not at present have a free hand and they certainly do prevent some crime, even if not all crime.

The second way of refuting a dilemma is to *go between the horns,* that is, to reject the second premise as not providing mutually exclusive alternatives. Our second premise was: either the police are given a free hand, *or* they are not given a free hand. The second half of the premise assumes that the police are completely restricted in what they do. However, there is a third alternative. We can place some restrictions on police behavior (eliminate the third degree, invoke *habeas corpus,* or insist on strict observance of the Miranda rule) but we give them some discretionary powers. This is in fact what we do.

The third way of refuting a dilemma is the most beautiful. Just as a dilemma was a very effective rhetorical device to end a series of objections, so a *counterdilemma* is a beautiful and effective way of dismissing the whole case of the opposition. First, look at the structure of the previous dilemma (above) and then note how a simple change below provides a foolproof formula for constructing a counterdilemma:

If . . . S_1 . . . then . . . not-S_4; *and* if . . . S_3 . . . then . . . not-S_2.

S_1 *or* S_3.

$\overline{}$

Therefore, not-S_4 *or* not-S_2.

In other words, what we have done is to reverse the order of S_2 and S_4 and negate them. What does the counterdilemma look like?

If the police are given a free hand, then they will prevent all crime (double negative here: original statement said not-prevent, here not-not-prevent is equivalent to prevent); and if they are not

not given a free hand, then they will *not* interfere with our civil liberties.

Either the police are given a free hand or they are not given a free hand. (Second premise remains the same.)

Therefore, the police must either prevent all crime *or* the police will not interfere with our civil liberties.

As you can see, the counterdilemma gives two equally attractive alternatives with the same information supplied by the original dilemma. It is effective against an opponent not because it really says anything, but because it shows you to be much more clever.

No discussion of dilemmas and counterdilemmas would be complete without including the famous example of the logic teacher and his pupil. The logic teacher advertised that any one of his students who lost his first court case would not have to pay the fee. Soon one of the students who completed the course announced outright that he refused to pay for the course of instruction. The logic teacher sued, taking the student to court.

In his defense the student argued: If I lose this case, then I do not have to pay the teacher (by advertisement); and if I win then I do not have to pay (by court decision). Either I win or I lose. Therefore, either I do not have to pay, or I do not have to pay. Either way I do not have to pay.

The teacher argued on his own behalf: If you win this case, then you must pay me (by advetisement); if you lose this case, then you must pay me (by court decision). Either you win this case or you lose this case. Therefore, either you pay me or you pay me. Either way you have to pay me.

Appeal to Self-interest

Just as in your presentation you pointed out some residual benefits of accepting your point of view, so in the defense of your presentation against your opponent's attacks you may repeat the appeal. However, here there should be a difference. In the presentation you appealed to some general interest shared by the whole, but here your appeal should be the very narrow self-interest of the immediate audience. For example, in a debate about the value of the United Nations let us suppose you present a list of all the values and accomplishments and promise of the world forum. Your opponent denigrates its actual accomplishments and even points out how much harm such an organization may do (e.g., easy access of spies to America). In your defense you will, of course, answer all of the objections worth answering. But there is no reason you cannot add an appeal to narrow self-interest. When speaking to a New York City audience you might as well point out how much money the United Nations contributes to the economy of the city. However, be wary of an opponent who appeals to self-interest by pointing out the city's expenses due to the United Nations, i.e., police protection.

WINNING THE ARGUMENT

The first stage of a successful defense is the repulsion of specific charges and assaults on your initial presentation. The second stage of defense is an attack on the alternatives. This is especially important if the first stage of your defense has not been as successful as you would have liked. Most arguments are won by showing that one side is better on balance, that is, has more assets and fewer liabilities.

However, if your original or first-stage defense has been successful, or if during the second stage of your defense you become successful, then an attack on the alternative position becomes a way of annihilating the enemy and winning the argument. In short, not only is your position defensible but theirs is not.

Damning the Alternative

Naturally enough, the first procedure in the move to win is called damning the alternative. There are three possibilities here: *(a)* if your opponent explicitly offers an alternative, attack it; *(b)* if your opponent only has an implicit position, bring his case out into the open and attack it; and *(c)* if he fails to offer any kind of alternative, then argue that there is no acceptable alternative to your position because if there were one then your opponent would have offered it. Thus you win by default.

As an example, we may take your defense of an "open society" (in the social, political, and economic sense). No doubt there are many shortcomings of an open society, but you can doubtlessly defend some of these as being either not really shortcomings or as necessary evils. For instance, in an open society there is competition and a great deal of wasteful controversy. However, this is a small price to pay for the great release of creative energy that this makes possible. But, in addition to your defense of an open society, you can honestly ask: what is the alternative? Aren't the so-called advantages of a totalitarian society illusory if not repressive? No defense of an open society has to deny that society's shortcomings; it has only to ask, is there a viable alternative?

Two Wrongs Make a Right

Any shortcoming of your position that cannot be defended can still be justified by pointing out the errors or shortcomings of the opposition. The difference between this technique and the one described above is the following. In the case of damning the alternative, you are claiming that on balance your position is better. In the case of "two wrongs make a right" you are claiming that certain apparent liabilities are really justified or caused by the errors of the opposition.

For example, let us imagine two countries at war. Country A has as its stated policy that torture is necessary and that the mass murder of civilians is necessary. In other words, atrocities are justified. Country B is opposed to atrocities. It does not excuse atrocities and when its soldiers commit them they are punished. Therefore, Country B is less likely to have atrocities committed by its personnel. This is a damning of the alternative.

On the other hand, when both countries resort to atrocities as a matter of policy, and not inadvertently on the part of some undisciplined soldiers, then we are not damning the alternative. When Country B says that its atrocities are justified because Country A resorts to atrocities, then the technique of "two wrongs make a right" is being used.

Another example of this is the suppression of the rights of free speech of some people on the grounds that those people themselves advocate censorship. For example, Communists do not advocate free speech in their views of what society should be. To deny them the rights of free speech in our society because they would deny free speech to us is to argue that two wrongs make a right.

Ad hominem

This most useful technique seems to appear everywhere. Instead of attacking the specific points of an argument, you attack the man. The special version to be used here is a way of making the audience believe that you have already successfully repulsed every part of your opponent's attack and now it is time to finish him off. This is like a postwar trial for the losers wherein you document the evil ways of the opponent. You tell your audience how someone falls into the trap of believing such nonsense.

Appeal to Ignorance

In this version we argue that because the opposition cannot prove its case, our case must be true be default.

For example, the Warren Commission's report on the assassination of John F. Kennedy has not convinced everyone, because there are loose ends in its evaluation of the evidence. The failure of the Warren Commission report to convince everyone beyond a shadow of a doubt automatically (so this technique would claim) means that those who have argued for a conspiracy are right. One of the major assumptions behind this technique is that the alternatives discussed are the only possible alternatives.

This technique is especially useful against any new idea or suggestion to adopt some policy that has never been tried before. If an idea has never been tried before, then obviously no one really knows if it is or will be a good one. Therefore, since we cannot prove it is good, it must be bad.

Invincible Ignorance and Falsification

In this form of attack on your opposition you accuse your opponent of clinging to principles or beliefs that he *(a)* accepts uncritically, *(b)* refuses to debate, and *(c)* offers no criteria for refutation or falsifiability.

There are people, for example, who believe in the Communist conspiracy, in the conspiracy of the military-industrial complex, or in the unbridgeable gap between management and labor, and they believe these things almost as matters of religious conviction. It is thus not the specific belief but the manner in which it is held that makes it subject to the charge of invincible ignorance. They refuse to listen to any criticism of their beliefs, they will not debate or discuss the matter, and, most important of all, they will not specify what would count against their belief.

The last criterion, falsifiability, is a critical one. It is almost a definition of rationality to say that a man is rational to the extent that he will tell you under what circumstances he will change his mind. To know when a belief will be considered false is to know how to reason with someone who holds that belief. It is a mark of psychosis that someone will not under any circumstances change his mind. To expose your opponent as one who holds this kind of belief is to undermine the audience's tolerance of him as a rational person.

Most people, of course, if given enough time and help, could specify when they would consider their beliefs disconfirmed. However, most people never really think about this point. You should take advantage of this lapse in attention and frequently charge your opponent with invincible ignorance. You will be surprised how often it will work.

Appeal to Force or Fear (*Ad baculum*)

There is no more effective technique for assuring your audience how much better your position is when compared to your opponent's than by pointing out the dire consequences that will follow the adoption of his proposal. Here you are appealing to fear.

An example of the appeal to fear is the claim or prediction made by insurance salesmen about the death of the father and the eventual suffering of the family. If all else fails, this fearful consequence will close the deal. What responsible father wants to think of his wife and children suffering after he has gone? After all, didn't this happen to so-and-so who lived around the corner . . .? In case the father is really hardhearted, the salesman, if he is any good, will elaborate this argument at length to the wife. Here a little forceful persuasion is in order.

Imagine the parents who say to their children, "Those of you who claim not to believe in Santa Claus will not get a Christmas present from him." This is a threat, however humorously or mythologically intended.

In arguments involving human behavior, one interesting element introduced into predictions of dire consequences is the possible threat of a self-fulfilling prophecy. Here you not only predict the dire consequence, but intimate in the most tactful way that you might even bring such a dire consequence about if your position is not adopted. For example, how often have you heard a spokesman for the blacks say, "If you do not improve the lot of the blacks and meet their demands there will be riots." How often have you heard the opponents of such demands say, "If you surrender to black extremist demands there will be a white backlash." Both of these statements are not just predictions but subtle threats.

Abandon Discussion

If you are absolutely convinced that you have overwhelmed your opponent, then you should cut off debate as soon as possible. To pursue the discussion beyond the point at which you have clearly won is to give your opponent an opportunity he does not deserve, it is to risk throwing away your victory, and it is to lend credibility to your opponent's case. Once you have won, cut off the discussion by saying something like, "I never argue with a man who is wrong!"

GOING FOR A TIE

Nobody wins them all. Not only will you have bad days but the opposition may just be lucky or the audience a bunch of complete dimwits. Hence you cannot expect to win them all. Suppose you have counterattacked as much as you could, and suppose you have tried to win but you simply cannot achieve a decisive and clear-cut victory, then what do you do? You go for a tie!

Do not admit defeat:
Under no circumstances should you admit defeat. Remember that there are three possible stages of your position: *(a)* you are completely right; or *(b)* you are mostly right but your position needs a few qualifications and corrections; or *(c)* you knowingly defended a weak position in order to dramatically call attention to a useful underlying principle.

True by definition:
You can always save your position by making it true by definition. This is not a victory. When you are forced to use this technique as a form of defense it always leaves the audience with the impression that your position was trivial and the argument almost a waste of time. But still this is better than losing. Suppose, for example, you have argued that abortion is always an act of murder. No matter what your opposition throws at you, you will always be right if you say you mean by murder the destruction of any living cell. The implications of this position might be pretty silly, e.g., destruction of plant life is murder, but you will at least be safe in your claim that abortion is murder.

Forestalling disagreement:
Perhaps a more effective technique when you must go for a tie is to argue that your opponent really agrees with your position. Thus there is no real argument and no real disagreement. This tactic is so surprising to some people that when, after having demolished their opponent, they find him claiming that everybody agrees, they fall right into the trap of being nice. Usually people who are interested in the truth fall into it.

The man who was most successful in using this technique was Paul Tillich, the famous theologian. He offered proofs of God's existence and arguments for a new view of religion. When attacked, and sometimes he was severely criticized and effectively refuted, he would fall back on the technique of arguing that the opponent really agreed. Even the opponent's respect for logic was in Tillich's view a sign of ultimate concern and therefore a proof of God's existence.

It is difficult to argue against this technique. The only way out is to keep insisting upon the differences in the positions. The risk you run when you try to wiggle out of someone else's use of forestalling disagreement is that you might alienate the audience. After all, he is trying to be nice and you are being a bastard. Here what you must do is restate the case of the one who is trying to forestall disagreement, restate it in such a manner that you appear the victor and welcome his repentance. For example, "As long as Tillich draws no moral or social implications from his position, as long as he admits his differences with traditional theology, and as long as he . . . then I welcome his conversion."

Invitation:
When you see that you cannot do anything else, give a summary of the progress of the argument, including the positions of both sides. Make this summary as positive and as friendly as possible. Organize it so that it looks as progressive as possible, that is, as if the argument has been heading progressively in a certain direction almost by prearrangement. Conclude with the remark that we have not come to the end or final determination, and *issue an invitation to your opponent to join you in the common search for the truth.*

Seven

Cause-and-Effect Reasoning

HISTORY OF THE CONCEPT OF 'CAUSATION'

The difficulties that surround the use of the concept of 'causation' can be best explained by examining its history. The oldest and most influential account was provided by Aristotle over two thousand years ago. According to Aristotle, the concept of 'causation' has to be understood in four different senses. That is, there are four kinds of causes:

(1) material cause
(2) formal cause
(3) efficient cause
(4) final cause.

The material cause is that out of which something is made or constructed; the formal cause refers to its internal structure; the efficient cause is that external agency from which the thing comes or originates; the final cause is the goal, function, or purpose of a thing.

When Aristotle applied this understanding of the four causes to man-made objects his analysis went as follows. A table, for example, is made of wood (material cause); it has the shape or form of a series of rectangles (formal cause); it was produced by a carpenter (efficient cause); and its purpose is to serve as a surface for such activities as eating and writing (final cause). The same kind of analysis can be applied to natural objects. For example, in the case of an acorn, its material cause is the organic substances that compose it; its efficient cause is an oak tree, namely, the parent oak tree; its formal cause is its structural potential to become an oak tree; and the final cause is to become another oak tree.

Something interesting thus distinguishes objects in nature from human actions, namely, the formal, final, and efficient causes turn out to be identical. The identity of the formal, final, and efficient causes allows anyone who uses Aristotle's theory on natural objects to infer backward from the effect to the cause as well as to infer forward from the cause to the effect. More accurately, to know something is to grasp its formal cause, and since the formal cause is identical to the final and efficient causes, to know something is to be able to infer where it came from and where it is going.

This principle of the identity of the formal, efficient, and final causes dominated Western thought for a very long time and was the basis of many important arguments. To illustrate this presence, let us look at Descartes's proof of God's existence. According to Descartes, we have an idea in our mind of a perfect being, namely, God. Where does this idea come from; that is, what is its cause? There are three possibilities: (1) the idea comes from our experience; (2) the idea was invented by man; (3) the idea was caused by something perfect, namely, God himself. Descartes argued by a process of elimination that (1) and (2) are false and therefore (3) must be true. Therefore, there is a God who causes us to have the idea (effect) of a perfect being.

In order for the elimination to succeed, Descartes must show that (1) and (2) are false. It is easy enough to dispose of (1). How does Descartes dispose of (2)? Man, according to Descartes, could not invent (cause) the idea of something perfect (an effect), because man is not himself perfect. The reason man would have to be perfect is that the efficient cause must be identical to the formal cause. That is, there cannot be anything or any property in the effect that is not already present in the cause. If the effect is perfect or has the property of 'perfection,' then the cause must have the property of 'perfection.'

Descartes, like those before him and like his contemporaries, employed Aristotle's conception of causation. However, this conception of causation was ultimately derived from Aristotle's physics. Ironically, one of the most important developments in modern physics (during the sixteenth and seventeenth centuries) was the displacement of Aristotelian physics by the theory of Isaac Newton. This, as we shall see, led to fundamental changes in our understanding and use of the concept of 'causation.'

The basic premise of Aristotelian physics has been that the state of rest is the natural state of an object. In Newtonian physics, on the other hand, motion is the natural state of an object. Just that one change leads in Newton's physics to the elimination of formal and final causes. In Newton's physics there are only efficient causes; thus, there cannot be any identity of formal, efficient, and final causes. Without that identity, there cannot be any backward inference from effect to cause without prior experience. David Hume was the first philosopher to comprehend the philosophical implications of the shift from Aristotelian physics to Newtonian physics, and he was able to show with great accuity the illegitimate use of all causal arguments based upon Aristotle's analysis of causation.

One of the reasons that Aristotle's analysis sounds so odd to the modern reader is that we are accustomed to using the concept of 'causation' in the single sense of efficient cause. This merely reflects the triumph of Newton's physics over that of Aristotle.

HUME'S DEFINITION OF CAUSE AND EFFECT

The clearest definition of the relationship between cause and effect (the reader is reminded that this is philosophically controversial) was provided by the great British philosopher David Hume (1711-1776). According to Hume we are justified in saying that thing is the cause (C) and another thing is the effect (E) if the following three conditions hold:

(1) C, the cause, *preceded* E, the effect, in time;

(2) C and E are *contiguous* in time and place; and

(3) there is a *history* of regularity in the precedence and contiguity of C and E.

Hume's analysis, of course, has to be qualified. He does this but I shall select only the part of it that concerns us here. We always talk about the cause preceding the effect for practical reasons. We want to be able to control events in advance so we look for conditions that take place prior in time to the event we want to control. Technically speaking, some causes are simultaneous with their effects, as when we say that the striking of the match is the cause of the match's lighting. It would be hair splitting to insist that the striking preceded the lighting in that there is clearly a sense in which both happen at the same time. Therefore we might be a little more accurate and say that the cause must precede, or be simultaneous with, the effect, or perhaps that no cause can follow the effect.

Second, there must be some more or less clear connection in time and space between the two events that we are connecting causally. We say that a specific fire is the cause of a specific effect, smoke, and we can see the smoke coming from that specific fire (space and time). When we say that a germ caused Mr. Smith to become ill, the germ and the illness both take place in Mr. Smith's body. Even when two distant events are causally related we speak of the intervening series of causes and effects forming a chain between the two events. For instance, the assassination of Archduke Franz Ferdinand at Sarajevo is a "cause" (allegedly) of World War I because of a whole series of intervening diplomatic and military events. Even where we do not know for sure the exact connection, we always suspect some kind of spatio-temporal link that we expect to discover later. No doubt the concept of contiguity would have to be redefined in terms of contemporary physics, but the everyday sense of it is well understood.

Third, and most important, is the history of regularity. Hume distinguishes between a natural psychological tendency to suspect a causal relation and the logical justification in believing there to be a causal connection (which depends upon a long history of regularity). For example, if while having dinner I drink some wine and the lights suddenly go out I may be psychologically tempted to think that my drinking wine causes lights to go out.

However, there is no past experience to justify this belief. The connection between turning the light switch and the lights going out has had such a long history of regularity that it would be irrational not to believe in their causal connection. It is the history of regularity that is usually crucial in settling conflicts over what caused what. This is why past experience is so important in documenting a case or position you want to defend.

CAUSAL REASONING AS PRACTICAL

In daily life we are interested in causes and effects in so far as they affect our lives. If we know the causes of things then we are in a better position to control what happens to us. This is behind the famous remark of Francis Bacon that "knowledge is power." The fact that cause and effect are practical concepts, concepts we employ in the practice of daily life, explains why the common man thinks more of technology than of science. Science is interested in concomitant variation, the relationships among "things" that can be described mathematically. Science is not interested in causation. Technology is the employment of scientific information to control the environment. Technology is very much an affair of cause and effect precisely because it introduces human purposes into the world of concomitant variation.

In practical life we are interested in events from two points of view: how to make things happen, i.e., how to bring them about, and how to prevent things from happening. For instance, as a farmer I want to know how to cause rain when my crops need it. That is, I would like to be able to "cause" rain for the convenience of my crops. At the same time, if possible, I would like to know how to prevent it from raining at times so as to prevent my crops from being ruined. That is, I want to know how to cause it not to rain.

In medicine we want to cure people, that is, to cause them to regain their health. We also want to prevent them from getting ill. Here we want to find the "causes" of disease and eliminate them. In political, social, and economic life we want to know the causes of human happiness so that we can nourish them, and the causes of human suffering so that we can eliminate them. To these two ends, bringing about and preventing, there correspond two technical concepts: sufficient and necessary conditions. In this context they will be defined as follows.

A *necessary condition* is a condition (state of affairs, thing, process, etc.) that must be present if we are to obtain the effect. One of the necessary conditions of life as we know it is oxygen. Some of the necessary conditions of a fire are oxygen, a flammable material, and a form of ignition. If we know the necessary conditions of an event then we can *prevent* it from happening. Remove any of the necessary conditions and the effect does not take place. Thus we can speak of a necessary condition as a cause, or one of the causes, of an event.

A *sufficient condition* is a condition (state of affairs, thing, process, etc.) that automatically leads to the production of another event. Swallowing cyanide is a sufficient condition for death. The difference between a necessary and a sufficient condition is that although a necessary condition must be present, by itself it will not produce the effect. The sufficient condition is "sufficient" by itself to produce the effect. Usually the sufficient condition is really a set of necessary conditions, all of which must be present at the same time and place. For instance, a combustible material, oxygen, and the combustion point are all necessary conditions for fire. Together all three constitute the sufficient conditions for a fire. If we know the sufficient condition of an event, then we can *produce* it at will. Thus we can speak of a sufficient condition as a cause of an event.

There are then at least two senses in which we talk about causes: causes as necessary conditions and causes as sufficient conditions. In addition, if we consider "cause" in the practical sense we can talk about *multiple causes*. Not only is swallowing cyanide a cause of death, but we can also die by getting a bullet in the heart. There is then a sense in which there can be more than one cause (of the sufficient variety) for an effect. When we talk about necessary conditions it is rather obvious that there can be more than one cause. Suppose one man shoots another. Suppose we want to know what would have prevented that effect. What is the cause? Without bullets there would have been no shooting; the same is true of a firing pin; the same is true of the gun, and so on back into the early childhood, no doubt, of the man who pulled the trigger. All of these are necessary conditions and therefore all of these events or things are causes.

There are several other ways in which causes and effects may be related. There is such a thing as a *causal chain*. For example, if A is the cause of B (where A may be a cause in either the necessary or sufficient condition sense) and B is the cause of C (where B may be a cause in either the necessary or sufficient condition sense), then in a very important sense we may also speak of A being a cause of C. For instance, if the presence of old newspapers in the basement of my house (newspapers are a combustible material and therefore a necessary condition of a fire) is a cause of my house catching fire, and if you are burned as an effect of that fire (fire is a sufficient condition of your being burned), then through the causal chain the newspapers are a cause of your being burned. Historians can make interesting use of causal chains, as when they say that had Cleopatra's nose been a half-inch longer the course of world history would have been different.

MILL'S METHODS

John Stuart Mill was a noted British philosopher and logician of the nineteenth century. In his famous work *System of Logic* (1843) he developed what he called "methods" for the analysis of causes and effects in specific situations. What follows is our translation of those methods into our previous scheme for discussing cause and effect.

Suppose you were interested in finding out which circumstances preceding an event or phenomenon (cause) or which circumstances following that event or phenomenon (effect) were really connected causally with that event or phenomenon. Mill suggests that we do this by comparing different instances of the event or phenomenon and then try to discover in what respects they agree and in what respects they differ.

Method of Agreement

"If two or more instances of the phenomenon under investigation have only one circumstance in common, the circumstance in which alone all of the instances agree is the cause (or effect) of the given pheonomenon."

Suppose you are giving a party at which various foods and beverages are served. After a while a number of people at the party begin to act strangely, that is, they talk very loudly, laugh at anything, begin to undress, and play various assorted pranks. In short, they are drunk. What caused these people at your party to get drunk? Was it the food? No, because everybody tasted the food and many did not get drunk. Was it the beverages? You examine the beverages and find that all of them are alcoholic (all beverages agree in having one circumstance in common) and all of the people who are inebriated drank the alcoholic beverages. Therefore, you may conclude that alocholic beverages caused people at your party to become drunk.

The method of agreement is effective because of certain assumptions and background information operative in any analysis. Mill has emphasized in his definition of the method that there is only one circumstance in common. For example, suppose the people who were drunk had had gin and soda, Scotch and soda, rum and soda, and various other mixed drinks containing soda. Then soda would be a circumstances in common. It is because we already know that soda does not cause drunkenness or because we may have eliminated it on the grounds that someone drank straight soda and did not get drunk that we are finally led to alcohol.

What the method of agreement does most effectively is to eliminate from consideration certain factors as not being necessary conditions for the production of an effect. For example, someone might think that standing under the mistletoe at the party is a cause of drunkenness. However, by finding a case of a person who is drunk but who did not stand under the mistletoe, we have a case of the phenomenon without the suspected condition being present. Since the effect can occur without that condition, then that condition (standing under the mistletoe) cannot be a necessary condition of being drunk.

Method of Difference

"If an instance in which the phenomenon under investigation occurs and an instance in which it does not occur have every circumstance in common save one, that one occurring only in the former, the circumstance in which alone the two instances differ is the effect, or the cause, or an indispensable part of the cause of the phenomenon."

Suppose a set of male twins boards a plane and sits together. Later during the plane trip one of them becomes violently ill. What is the cause? The answer is found by locating one condition that is different when there are no other differing conditions. Both have the same general health, performed the same activities before boarding the plane, sat in the same area (they even periodically exchanged seats). The stewardess, however, remembers that everyone on the plane including one of the twin brothers had steak for lunch, whereas the other twin was the only person who had something else for lunch (lobster). Since this is the only circumstance in which they differ then the lobster lunch must be the cause of the man's illness.

What the method of difference does most effectively is to eliminate from consideration certain factors as not being sufficient conditions for the production of an effect. For example, someone might have argued that the before-lunch cocktail on the plane might have been the cause of the illness. However, since both men had a cocktail and one of them did not get sick, then having the cocktail does not lead by itself automatically to getting sick. Hence the cocktail is not a sufficient condition for causing the illness on the plane.

Joint Method of Agreement and Difference

"If two or more instances in which the phenomenon occurs have only one circumstance in common, while two or more instances in which it does not occur have nothing in common save the absence of that circumstance, the circumstance in which alone the two sets of instances differ is the effect, or the cause, or an indispensable part of the cause, of the phenomenon."

Suppose you were at a party where five kinds of punch were prepared and each punch had its ingredients marked on its respective bowl. All together there were five ingredients:

    A. cranberry juice
    B. orange slices
    C. sugar
    D. seltzer
    E. rye whiskey

The five punches had different combinations and only some of the punches tasted good. What was the "cause" of the good taste? Let us schematize the available combinations and assume that no further experimentation is possible.

    Punch 1 ingredients: ABC E (good taste)
    Punch 2 ingredients: A   DE (good taste)
    Punch 3 ingredients: B DE (good taste)
    Punch 4 ingredients: A C   (*bad* taste)
    Punch 5 ingredients: B D   (*bad* taste)

To review, punch 5 had only orange slices and seltzer in it. Looking at the first two punches, we could not use the method of agreement. However, when we take into account punch 3 we can see by the method of agreement that E, rye whiskey, might be the cause of good taste. Can we use the method of difference to check out if the absence of rye whiskey will lead to bad taste? Only if we can make two punches with everything in common except E can we use the method of difference. However, we cannot use it here, because while punches 4 and 5 lack E they are different in too many other respects, However, the joint method does tell us that E is the cause (necessarily) of the good taste. Thus the joint method works when the method of difference cannot be used. The joint method eliminates D, B, C, and A as necessary conditions of good tasting punch, and it eliminates A, C, B, and D as sufficient conditions of good tasting punch.

FALLACIES OF CAUSAL REASONING

As a result of the two previous sections, all of the following fallacies concerning causal reasoning will appear to be due either to a violation of Hume's three criteria of cause and effect or to a violation of Mill's methods concerning the elimination of necessary and sufficient conditions.

Concomitant Variation

This is the fallacy of assuming that because two events show a high incidence of correlation they are therefore causally connected. This is especially true of statistical correlations. For example, the rapid increase of college enrollments during the decade of the 1920s varies concomitantly with rapid increase in the number of inmates in institutions for the mentally ill. Is there a causal connection? Hardly. This variation satisfies none of Hume's criteria: there is no indication of which event preceded which, there is no connection seen or imaginable between these events spatially, and no history of regularity prior to the decade of the 1920s.

Statistical correlation between lung cancer and cigarette smoking is acceptable as an instance of causal reasoning because it does satisfy the criteria: cigarette smoking precedes lung cancer, independent research on the effects of nicotine on the skin of mice makes a spatial connection imaginable, and there is now a long history of such correlation.

What about the relationship between night and day? Doesn't day follow night and night day with unerring regularity? Does this mean that night causes day or does day cause night? The answer is obvious: while night and day do satisfy the two criteria of a history of regularity and spatial connection, they do not satisfy the criterion of temporal priority, because we cannot tell whether night precedes day or whether day regularly precedes night. Since no one can say, then we do not have the right to say that either one does and therefore the example does not fit the three criteria.

There is another famous example called the example of the occasionalist clocks. Imagine two clocks, A and B, where allegedly clock A is five minutes ahead of clock B. Every hour on the hour the clocks chime. Since A regularly chimes before B, does this imply that A is the cause of B?

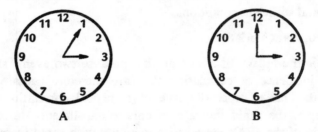

The diagram is useful because it shows that it is impossible to state any general relation of temporal priority between the two clocks. Clock A may be viewed as five minutes ahead of clock B, but clock B may also be viewed as eleven hours and fifty-five minutes ahead of clock A. Consequently, the example of the two clocks does not meet the requirement of temporal priority. In addition, there is no spatial connection between the two clocks.

Known Counterexample

The following fallacy is committed, so far as I know, only by philosophers and logicians. Imagine that at twelve o'clock a siren goes off at a factory signaling the lunch hour. At the same time a train leaves the railroad station every day at the noon hour. Does the siren cause the train to leave? The example would seem to fit the criteria of temporal precedence and historical regularity. However, to begin with there is no clear spatial connection. More important, the example really does not fit the criterion of historical regularity since all of us already know from past experience (*a*) that the siren does not cause the train to depart and (*b*) that if the siren did not go off the train would depart anyway; that is, we know the real cause of the train's departure.

It should be noted that the examples of night and day and the occasionalist clocks are also examples of the fallacy of known counterexample.

Post Hoc

The original Latin expression is *"post hoc, ergo propter hoc,"* which when translated means "after this, therefore because of this." It is a fallacy of causal reasoning in that it is based on the mistaken belief that mere temporal priority constitutes a causal relation. It completely neglects the other criteria of spatial connection and a history of regularity.

There are some amusing and some not so amusing examples of the *post hoc* fallacy. For example, Mrs. Smith prays that her husband will recover from the mumps and he does. She assumes that since the prayer preceded the recovery then the prayer must be the cause of the recovery.

In advertising, this sort of fallacy appears quite frequently. There are endless testimonials about how people recovered after taking Dr. Hippocrates' snake oil. Without some other evidence of a connection and some historical laboratory evidence there is no good reason to believe that the snake oil really was the cause of the recovery. We all know that cold remedies cure a cold in seven days and that without the remedy the cold takes a week to go away.

Irreversible Order

Here we shall begin discussing examples of fallacies in causal reasoning that violate some of Mill's methods by confusing and misusing distinctions between necessary and sufficient conditions. The fallacy of irreversible order is based on the assumption that if A causes B, then B cannot be the cause of A. For example, the existence of poverty in some countries prevents them from sponsoring universities and even simple programs to raise the literacy rate. Thus clearly *poverty is a cause of ignorance.* At the same time, there are historical examples of how the closing of the universities (e.g., Spain and Italy during the Inquisition) led eventually to impoverishing the economy as a whole. Thus, clearly, *ignorance can cause poverty.* In terms of the distinction between necessary and sufficient conditions, the fallacy of irreversible order incorrectly assumes that if A is a sufficient condition of B, then B cannot be a sufficient condition for A.

Denying the Antecedent

The best way to see this fallacy is to show first a correct argument and then an incorrect one using the fallacy.

> If you take cyanide *then* you will die.
> *You take cyanide.*
> _____
> *Therefore,* you will die.

Schematically the argument looks like this:

> $If . . .S_1 . . . then . . . S_2.$
> $S_1.$
> _____
> *Therefore,* $S_2.$

Now let us look at an incorrect form of the argument.

> If you take cyanide then you will die.
> You do *not*-take cyanide.
> _____
> Therefore, you will *not*-die.

Schematically the argument looks like this.

> $If . . . S_1 . . . then . . . S_2.$
> $Not\text{-}S_1.$
> _____
> Therefore, not-S_2.

You can now see the difference between the two arguments. A sentence of the form "if . . . then" is called a conditional sentence. The part of the conditional sentence following the "if" is called the antecedent. In the second example above, the antecedent is denied and that is why it is called denying the antecedent. Now it should be intuitively obvious that the second example is an example of poor or fallacious reasoning, whereas the first example is a true example of causal reasoning. Why? The answer is simple. The second example is wrong because there are other causes of death besides swallowing cyanide. Even if I do not take cyanide I will eventually die some other way. In terms of necessary conditions, the *fallacy of denying the antecedent is the fallacy of believing that* S_1 *(cyanide) is a necessary condition* of death *when* in actuality *it is a sufficient condition.*

Affirming the Consequent

This fallacy is very similar to the one we discussed above. We are still dealing with conditional sentences (if . . . then) and the part of the conditional sentence following the "then" is called the consequence. We can use the same example.

> *If* I take cyanide *then* I die.
> I die.
> _____
> *Therefore* I took cyanide.

Schematically the argument looks like this:

> *If* . . . S_1 . . . *then* . . . S_2
> S_2.
> _____
> *Therefore,* S_1.

The correct scheme, you will recall, is:

> *If* . . . S_1 . . . *then* . . . S_2.
> S_1.
> _____
> *Therefore,* S_2.

The difference between the two schemes is obvious. In the fallacious one, we have reversed the order of S_1 and S_2. We have *affirmed the consequent,* hence the name of the fallacy, when we should have affirmed the antecedent. The fact that I died does not automatically imply that I took cyanide even if the first sentence about cyanide causing death is true. Obviously there are other causes of death besides cyanide. Actually, in terms of necessary and sufficient conditions the error here is the same as the error of denying the antecedent; it is the *fallacy of assuming that a sufficient condition is a necessary one*. Cyanide is a sufficient condition of dying but not a necessary one.

Genetic Fallacy

We have already seen several examples of genetic arguments, an argument or explanation of how a belief came about or how someone comes to believe something. Such explanations, when true, are perfectly legitimate, useful, and enlightening. There is, however, a special form of this argument that is quite fallacious.

Suppose I argue that the presence of oxygen in a forest preserve was *the* cause of a forest fire. Now it is true that if there had been no oxygen in the forest there certainly would have been no forest fire. It is also true that if there had been no lightning or a dropped match or whatever, there would have been no forest fire. In other words, when it is assumed that one of several necessary conditions was the sole and exclusive cause of an effect we have a genetic fallacy.

The same kind of fallacy is found when one excuses a criminal for his crime on the grounds that (genetically and necessarily) he committed his crime as a result of environmental factors. In reply we may note that the legal system (genetically and necessarily) must find the defendant guilty and punish him. We would have to "understand" the judge, jury, prosecutor, and executioner because they, too, are victims of their environment. Perhaps a more interesting question is not what caused the crime, but what would be the effect of punishing or not punishing the defendant.

PROBLEMS WITH THE CONCEPT OF 'CAUSATION'

Hume's analysis of causation is based upon a Newtonian, mechanical account of the physical world. Aristotle's analysis had been based not upon a physical-mechanical-deterministic model of the world but upon a teleological (purposive) account. Because all of Aristotle's world was entirely teleological (goal-directed) and not deterministic, Aristotle's analysis of 'causation' applied equally to human beings and to physical events. Therefore, it did not seem strange to talk about causes with regard to human action, to distinguish the different kinds or categories of causation, and it was still possible to uphold the general view that human beings are agents responsible for their actions.

Starting with Hume himself, many thinkers have tried to apply the new mechanical conception of 'causation' to human action. The problem with this application is that it denies that human beings are agents responsible for their own actions, and it seems to mean that human actions are the result of internal forces, external forces, or both, which are ultimately beyond human control or the desire to control them. Beginning with Hume and continuing to the present, philosophers have (a) tried to reconcile human agency with the mechanical view of causation, (b) happily abandoned the notion of human agency altogether, or (c) denied that the new mechanical view of causation applied to man.

This is not the context in which we can review all of the philosophical dimensions of this controversy. However, the reader should keep the following in mind. First, it is an open question and by no means settled whether the mechanical view of causation applies to human beings. No one has ever produced a single example of a case where we can show the necessary and sufficient conditions of human action. Second, in order to apply the mechanical view of causation to human, action it has been necessary since the time of Hume himself to ignore the criterion of spatial contiguity between cause and effect simply because we have no idea how this operates with people. As a consequence, all attempts to use the mechanical view of causation could be said to be guilty of the *post hoc* fallacy or perhaps others as well. Therefore, we must treat with both caution and some skepticism the widespread use of the mechanical view of causation by such social scientists as psychologists and sociologists. When it is alleged that watching violent films "causes" children to act in a violent manner or that poverty "causes," crime we must be careful in accepting this kind of interpretation.

When we are discussing a physical event it makes sense to use the mechanical concept of 'causation'. In such cases there is a natural necessity: given certain conditions (like the presence of oxygen and a high enough temperature) and given the absence of interfering conditions, an object will burn. The conditions are jointly sufficient to cause the effect, we can deduce the effect from the cause, and we can rationally make predictions based upon the information.

As soon as we come to biological phenomena the situation is already more complicated. Biological or organic systems, unlike textbook cases of physical systems, exist in time as well as in space. That is, organic phenomena are in a constant state of exchange with their surrounding environmental conditions. For example, whatever the exact relation between smoking and cancer turns out to be, it is not a simple and straightforward example like physical-mechanical causation. There are, for example, lots of heavy smokers who do not develop lung cancer, and those smokers who stop have different experiences depending upon when they stop smoking. Analogously, there are people with natural immunities to certain diseases and others who are allergic to substances that the rest of us find harmless.

When we move to the level of human action the situation might be altogether different. Again, without prejudicing the issue, let me sketch a view that can talk about human causation without denying human agency and freedom. That is, we are going to argue that in the case of human beings there are no socio-physiological stimuli sufficient to cause all human action. Here we shall return to some of the elements in Aristotle's analysis.

material cause	- human physiology
formal cause	- social meaning of an action
final cause	- meaning to the agent
efficient cause	- agent's decision

While physiology is an important factor it is not the sole determining factor of human action. Certainly a damaged physiological system or a system under the influence of externally induced chemical changes can malfunction and make certain actions impossible. But we cannot conclude from this that all action is totally the result of physiological factors. To believe otherwise is to argue fallaciously.

> All times that Smith is drunk are times that he
>   behaves obnoxiously.
> Now is a time Smith is behaving obnoxiously.
> _____
> Therefore, now is a time Smith is drunk.

The foregoing argument is a clear case of the fallacy of affirming the consequent.

With regard to formal causality or social meaning, we are in a position to deal with how the social context can influence, or be a factor in, human action. This also means that, with regard to human action, we must take the social perspective into account. But here we must also note that the "same" event might have different meanings to the people involved. For example, a final examination in school has different meanings for the administration, the instructor, and the students. Thus there can be conflicting accounts of the meaning of an event or action. Some of us would even want to discount the alleged existence of some social meanings such as "witches," "Jewish conspiracies," and the like. There are no clear behavioral criteria for identifying social meaning. For example, an employer refuses to hire a black applicant. Without further information, it would be ludicrous to identify this as an act of discrimination.

The final cause is the personal meaning that the agent gives to his action. In order to understand why an agent performs an action we must know what the action means to that agent. But in the end, it could be argued, the agent is responsible for the personal meaning he attaches to an action, and this is the efficient cause of an action. For example, a young man who lacks certain skills (material cause) and for whom few or no opportunities exist in the job market (formal cause) may turn to a life of crime because he is too proud to go back to school (final cause). We could explain the criminal behavior by reference to either the material cause, the formal cause, or the final cause. Yet if the agent's decision (efficient cause) in his choice of personal meaning (the "pride" that serves as the final cause) is one for which he is responsible, then he is responsible regardless of the presence of material and formal causes. If someone argues that the agent's choice of personal meaning is totally the result of external forces, then it would make no sense to hold him responsible. Keep in mind that this issue is far from being resolved.

Appendix

The following is intended as a tool, a reading guide, for helping the reader to ask the right kind of questions when reading a work designed to present an argument. Not only will these questions, when raised in appropriate circumstances, improve reading comprehension, but they should also help to develop more analytical and critical perspective on argumentative works.

I. What is the *problem?*
  A. How is this problem formulated?
  B. Why is this problem an important one?
  C. What is the history of this problem?
  D. Which prominent personalities have been interested in this problem?

II. What *solutions* to the problem are there?
  A. What are the conclusions reached?
  B. By what argument(s) is the conclusion reached?
  C. What facts or assumptions serve as premises?
  D. When a prominent personality offers a solution, does he also argue for or against other prominent personalities?
     Does he raise objections to alternative solutions?
     Does he consider objections to his own solutions?

III. *Evaluation*
  A. What are the advantages and disadvantages of the alternative formulations to the problem?

B. Has the importance or history of the problem ever
   been misrepresented?
C. Are the solutions logically related to the premises?
D. Are the facts true? Are the assumptions acceptable?
   Are the objections answerable?

I. WHAT IS THE PROBLEM?

Every work is concerned with a particular problem, issue, or
controversy. The choice of a word is not important here as long
as the readers ask themselves what is the particular issue or set of
issues about which the work is written. Until the reader uncovers
this issue his reading is either pointless or undirected. Sometimes
that issue is stated explicitly, and sometimes it is only implicit.
Sometimes that issue is stated in the first paragraph, and sometimes it is buried deep within the work. When the latter prevails,
the reader must search for it, and perhaps even reread the work
once it is found. But until you can state exactly what problem is
being dealt with, your reading is merely tentative, hypothetical,
and should be pursued cautiously.

Not every author would win the Nobel prize for literature,
anymore than every freshman essay belongs in the literary hall of
fame. Some are notoriously poor writers, and this should be kept
in mind so that readers do not feel that all of the problem is
theirs.

A. *How is the problem formulated?* Law students are familiar with the old joke of the attorney who, while cross-examining a
witness, asked: "Have you stopped beating your wife? Answer
'yes' or 'no.'" Either way the witness would be admitting that he
had beaten his wife in the past. This, of course, may not be true,
but the clever attorney will have tried to embarrass the witness by
asking his question in a particular way. The moral of this story is
that *how a question is asked determines the kind of answer you
can expect.* More important, you will discover that what distinguishes one author from another, one philosophical style from
another, is the manner in which questions are asked.

This is largely what is meant by saying that the question is more important than the answer. It does not mean that we are uninterested in the answer; on the contrary, most of us are passionately involved with answers. It means that the answer is implicitly structured by the question and how it is asked.

It also means that the sophisticated reader must be aware of the fact that there are alternative ways of asking a question, and the alternatives have momentous consequences. In the beginning when you have read only one or even a few authors, it will be difficult to think about alternatives, but after you have become familiar with several alternatives it will be easy to conceive of others. For example, after you have read Plato and Aristotle, you may read Descartes. While reading Descartes and noting how he asks questions you will automatically ask yourself, "How would Plato have viewed that question? How would Aristotle handle that issue?" and so on. The more background knowledge you accumulate, both in philosophy and in other fields, the more possibilities will occur. After a while, the only limitation will be your own imagination.

B. *Why is this problem an important one?* Questions do not arise in a vacuum. There is a reason why, when, where, and how they occur. We say that the problem exists in a certain context, and that the context structures the problem, which is another way of saying that how the question is asked determines the answer. Knowing the background to a question is essential to understanding it. It is interesting that even professional philosophers disagree with each other because they approach the same essay with different background assumptions, and that there have been major shifts in the interpretation of classical works with the discovery of more background information.

In addition to the background, there is the all-important element of how the author sees his own problem. A clear writer will not only state the problem but he will also try to indicate just why he thinks that the problem is important enough to deserve his energies as an author, and to be worthy of the reader's attention. Spotting this element helps you to comprehend the issue and its solution. Problems are important for many reasons, all the way from the survival of the human race (and you will be surprised at how many philosophers have this foremost in mind) to seeemingly technical issues that might appear to be of interest only to specialists. Even in the latter case, these technical issues are usually related to very practical concerns. Finally, it will be interesting to see how what looks like the same problem takes on an interesting history, because in different ages the same problem may be important but for different reasons.

C. *What is the history of this problem?* Not only will the careful writer state his personal reasons for believing the problem to be important, but he will also indicate the history of the problem. Usually the same problem has appeared before, or at least has been treated by other authors. Some reference to this history or previous treatment is usually made. For the moment we are not concerned with how accurately the history of the problem has been portrayed. Rather, we are concerned with how the author "sees" the history of the problem. In some cases you might want to point out that the author "does not see." We may even grant that authors, especially the greatest, are frequently unfair to their predecessors and colleagues. We grant all this for the moment because what is of interest here is how the *author's personal preconceptions help structure the way in which he has asked his question.* We must always try to understand the author first from his own interior point of view. Even if we later criticize that point of view, our criticism will be fair if we have first made a sincere attempt to see from that point of view.

D. *What prominent personalities have been interested in this problem?* Everything said above applies to this question as well. Authors will often mention other authors either explicitly or implicitly. Knowing those other works helps to understand the work you are reading at the moment.

You may address posterity but you can only answer the past. Moreover, authors not only read other authors but they react to general intellectual climates as well. You will be surprised by how much is a response to developments in the sciences. The same can be said for artistic, political, social, and religious developments.

II. What *solutions* to the problem are there?

After you have identified the problem or set of problems about which the author is writing, you will be in a position to look for the answer or answers he provides. When looking for the solution, the following should be kept in mind.

A. *What are the conclusions reached?* Although we have stated matters in the form of questions and answers, we should bear in mind that there are at least three possibilities.

(1) *A direct answer:* An author may have a direct answer to give to a specific problem. If so, you should look for it and state it.

(2) *Dissolving the problem:* Another possibility is the case where the author declares the problem to be a pseudo-problem; that is, no problem at all. For example, an old standby in philosophy is the question, What came first—the chicken or the egg? This question is exemplary of the Aristotelian problem of the cause of motion. In Aristotle's physics, rest is the natural state and motion is what has to be explained. The very beginning of motion, or of anything, is what an Aristotelian philosopher concerns himself with. To him, the question is important. On the contrary, in Newtonian physics, motion is a natural state, so that one can never meaningfully ask what causes motion. The very beginning of anything is not a serious issue if we take Newton's physics as our standard, and this is just exactly what Hume did. Hence, in Hume the question of most concern to an Aristotelian would be dismissed as meaningless.

It is not our purpose here to decide on the relative merits of competing theories of physics, or whether Aristotle or Hume is correct. We are concerned with pointing out how a question can seem vital to a philosopher who looks out on the world from one point of view, and how that same question can appear to be no question at all to a philosopher with another point of view. If we have prepared our ground in asking the right question about what the problem is, then we shall be able to anticipate the maneuvering that goes on in finding the solution.

(3) *Plea for recognition:* Sometimes an author will not have a solution to a particular problem. Rather, it will be his purpose to point out that the problem exists. In itself this can be a great contribution since we cannot solve problems if we do not know that they exist, and even then we must be able to recognize them in time.

B. *By what argument(s) is the conclusion reached?* In many ways this is the most interesting question for the logician. While most people think it sufficient simply to know the conclusions of this or that particular author, it is much more vital to know the reasons behind the conclusion. By *reasons* here we do not mean motives, but those logical considerations which lead to the adoption of the conclusion. Why is this so?

First, we may agree with the conclusion but not with the argument behind it. A bad argument may lose support for an otherwise acceptable conclusion. Second, we may disagree with the conclusion but find the argument powerful or useful for other purposes. Finally, by understanding the arguments we may be able to extend them to other contexts that the original author never considered. In short, we can learn from the argument more than we can from the conclusion.

Moreover, if we are to be rational men and women, then presumably we will want to defend our conclusions as rational and not merely accepted as a matter of blind faith. It is not enough to complain about the irrationality of others and then refuse to make the effort to be rational oneself.

An argument will be said to have the following structure: one or more premises and one conclusion. The *conclusion* is that which the author is trying to prove. The *premises* are those beliefs which the author gives as reason for accepting the conclusion.

C. *What facts or assumptions serve as the premises?* The premises are those reasons offered in support of the conclusion. Authors usually appeal to those beliefs which they think that their audience already accepts and then try to show that the favored conclusion also follows from those beliefs or is at least consistent with those beliefs.

In different historical periods and places different beliefs prevail. Many arguments are thus "dated" in the sense that what is acceptable in one time or place is not necessarily acceptable in another. Presumably, this holds for some of our own favorite beliefs as well.

There is another distinction worth making, as long as it is not made too sharply. We may distinguish between facts and assumptions. Facts are those alleged beliefs which we feel can be easily checked against experience, such as the color of an object, the temperature of a liquid, or the date of someone's birth. Assumptions are those beliefs which either cannot be checked directly, or are in principle not the sorts of things that can be checked. For example, the temperature in the center of the sun is not checkable, at least now, because no thermometer could withstand the heat. More interestingly, the belief that the future will resemble the past or the belief that mankind will one day understand everything, are not really checkable at all. Such assumptions guide our thinking about other things. Philosophers are very much concerned with the status of such *ultimate* premises. For our purposes at this stage it is only important to try to recognize when an author is stating a fact that he believes can be checked, and when he is appealing to an ultimate premise.

D. *What alternatives are considered?* Authors not only present arguments for their own solutions but also raise objections against alternative solutions. Frequently the case for one's conclusion is not so much its own strength but the weakness of alternative views. In line with this, the reader must learn to ask:

does the author argue for or against the solutions of other authors? Does he raise objections to those solutions, and if so what are they? Does he consider objections to his own solution? A wise writer anticipates the kinds of responses he will receive and tries to meet these objections before they can ever be articulated.

A good deal of logical reading involves the laying out of both the author's own position and his consideration of alternative positions. Here it is important to keep asking yourself as you read, "Is the author speaking for himself or is he reporting the viewpoint of the opposition?" This is part of the dialectic of logical argument, and mastering it is the key to successful comprehension.

III. *Evaluation*

Students frequently ask, "Do you want us to summarize the author or do you want our opinion?" Putting the question this way presupposes that the two activities are distinct. It also presupposes a rather naive view of presenting one's own opinion. I would point out that it is impossible to "summarize" another philosopher without raising some evaluative questions. In fact, without evaluation you cannot really be said to comprehend. Then again, it is impossible to evaluate without fully comprehending. I think that if the reader makes an attempt to comprehend an author in the manner suggested by Parts I and II of the outline, then he will already have been engaged in an evaluative process. Let us spell this out.

A. Look at IA. *What are the advantages or disadvantages of the alternative formulations of the problem?* Once you have become aware of the alternative formulations, that is, once you have read at least two authors, you can at the very least use one against the other. You might even want to use each against the other in order to suggest a third possibility.

B. Look at IB and IC. *Has the importance or history of the problem been misrepresented?* Maybe the problem is no longer important, or maybe it is important for totally new reasons. Maybe a better knowledge of the history of the problem leads to a different solution. It is not only in Orwell's *1984* that history is systematically distorted. It is even possible that what a classical author said many years ago caused or influenced the problem to change in the meantime. Finally, we risk pointing out that the way one interprets the history of anything is symptomatic of a particular philosophical point of view.

C. Look at IIC. *Do you agree with the facts appealed to?* As we have already pointed out, the conclusions follow from the premises. If you do not like the conclusion, then you must reject either one or more of the facts alleged or the assumptions made. Here, expressing a dissenting opinion can be a logically sophisticated response on your part, and not just an emotional reaction.

D. Look at IID. *Are the objections answerable?* Here there are several possibilities. If author A attacks author B, and you agree with author B, then why not try to show how author B would respond? That is, respond on his behalf. The fact that an author is attacked does not imply that the attack is a good one, and you can show how it has failed. Moreover, the fact that an author considers objections in advance of his solution does not mean that he has successfully answered them. If you feel that the reply is insufficient, offer a rebuttal of your own. Finally, if you agree with an author, you may want to present additional arguments in support of his case, for he may not have been in a position to consider them. By the time you have done all this, your reading will not be a mere summary or a simple-minded personal opinion but a kind of logical thinking in its own right.

John Stuart Mill:
On Liberty—Text and Analysis

1. The subject of this Essay is not the so-called Liberty of the Will, so unfortunately opposed to the misnamed doctrine of Philosophical Necessity; but Civil, or Social Lib-

erty; the nature and limits of the power which can be legitimately exercised by society over the individual, a question seldom stated, and hardly ever discussed, in general terms, but which profoundly influences the practical controversies of the age by its latent presence, and is likely soon to make itself recognized as the vital question of the future. It is so far from being new, that in a certain sense, it has divided mankind, almost from the remotest ages; but in the stage of progress into which the more civilized portions of the species have now entered, it presents itself under new conditions, and requires a different and more fundamental treatment.

Paragraph 1: "The subject of this essay is . . . civil, or social liberty: the nature and limits of the power which can be legitimately exercised by society over the individual." Mill immediately informs his readers of the *problem* with which he will be dealing. This corresponds to (I) in the reading guide outline. (IA) *How is the problem formulated?* The formulation of the problem involves a contrast: *society* on the one hand and the *individual* on the other. Mill thus makes a sharp distinction between the individual and society. As we shall discover later, other philosophers will not agree with this separation. As a reader of English you probably take this distinction as obvious, but that is a result of the fact that Mill represents the mainstream of Anglo-Saxon thought. It should also be noted that Mill is not asking about the present limits (a sociological question) but what *ought* to be the limits, legitimately; that is a moral question. Finally, we note that Mill does not mention the government, rather, he mentions society.

(IB) *Why is this problem an important one?* Mill notes that this problem has a long history which he will discuss shortly. But he claims that there are "new conditions" which "require a different and more fundamental treatment." What these circumstances are he does not discuss in this paragraph. See paragraphs 3, 4, and 15.

2. The struggle between Liberty and Authority is the most conspicuous feature in the portions of history with which we are earliest familiar, particularly in that of Greece, Rome, and England. But in old times this contest was between subjects, or some classes of subjects, and the government. By liberty was meant protection against the tyranny of the political rulers. The rulers were conceived (except in some of the popular governments of Greece) as in a necessarily antagonistic position to the people whom they ruled. They consisted of a governing One, or a governing tribe or caste, who derived their authority from inheritance or conquest, who, at all costs, did not hold it at the pleasure of the governed, and whose supremacy men did not venture, perhaps did not desire to contest, whatever precautions might be taken against its oppressive exercise. Their power was regarded as necessary, but also as highly dangerous; as a weapon which they would attempt to use against their subjects, no less than against external enemies. To prevent the weaker members of the community from being preyed upon by innumerable vultures, it was needful that there should be an animal of prey stronger than the rest, commissioned to keep them down. But as the king of the vultures would be no less bent upon preying on the flock, than any of the minor harpies, it was indispensable to be in a perpetual attitude of defense against his beak and claws. The aim, thereof patriots, was to set limits to the power which the ruler should be suffered to exercise over the community; and this limitation was what they meant by liberty. It was attempted in two ways. First, by obtaining a recognition of certain immunities, called political liberties or rights, which it was to be regarded as a breach of duty in the ruler to infringe, and which if he did infringe, specific resistance, or general rebellion, was held to be justifiable. A second, and generally a later expedient, was the establishment of constitutional checks; by which the consent of the community or of a body of some sort, supposed to represent its interests, was made a necessary condition to some of the more important acts of the governing power.

To the first of these modes of limitation, the ruling power, in most European countries, was compelled, more or less, to submit. It was not so with the second; and to attain this, or when already in some degree possessed, to attain it more completely, became everywhere the principle object of the lovers of liberty. And so long as mankind were content to combat one enemy by another, and to be ruled by a master, on condition of being guaranteed more or less efficaciously against his tyranny, they did not carry their aspirations beyond this point.

Paragraph 2: In this paragraph, Mill gives his version of the *history of the problem* (IC). His history refers to three countries: *Greece, Rome* (of the Republican period, not the Empire), and *England.* His history is limited to those times and places relevant to the history of modern England (and the U.S. by extension) since he is writing for a specific audience. Obviously, referring to other times and places would produce a different history. In these examples, the *problem* of the individual versus society was understood in terms of an adversary relationship: "The rulers were conceived . . . as in a necessarily antagonistic position to the people whom they ruled." Some of our contemporary talk of the government as the "they" in "Washington" preserves the flavor of this history. In short, rulers were necessary evils. The individual was protected in two ways: (1) a doctrine of "rights" and (2) "constitutional checks." The U.S. Constitution with its Bill of Rights, as well as the doctrine of checks and balances, is a perfect example of this. The U.S. Constitution was the product of the eighteenth century and the previous influence upon the founding fathers of Hobbes, Locke, Hume, and Montesquieu. Mill was writing in the nineteenth century, and was an heir of that tradition. (ID)

3. A time, however, came, in the progress of human affairs, when men ceased to think it a necessity of nature that their governors should be an independent power, opposed in interest to themselves. It appeared to them much better

that the various magistrates of the State should be their tenants or, delegates, revocable at their pleasure. In that way alone, it seemed, could they have complete security that the powers of government would never be abused to their disadvantage. By degrees, this new demand for elective and temporary rulers became the prominent object of the exertions of the popular party, wherever any such party existed; and superseded, to a considerable extent, the previous efforts to limit the power of rulers. As the struggle proceeded for making the ruling power emanate from the periodical choice of the ruled, some persons began to think that too much importance had been attached to the limitation of the power itself. *That* (it might seem) was a resource against rulers whose interests were habitually opposed to those of the people. What was now wanted was, that the rulers should be identified with the people; that their interest and will should be the interest and will of the nation. The nation did not need to be protected against its own will. There was no fear of its tyrannizing over itself. Let the rulers be effectually responsible to it, promptly removable by it, and it could afford to trust them with power of which it could itself dictate the use to be made. Their power was but the nation's own power, concentrated, and in a form convenient for exercise. This mode of thought, or rather perhaps of feeling, was common among the last generation of European liberalism, in the Continental section of which, it still apparently predominates. Those who admit any limit to what a government may do, except in the case of such governments as they think ought not to exist, stand out as brilliant exceptions among the political thinkers of the Continent. A similar tone of sentiment might by this time have been prevalent in our own country, if the circumstances which for a time encouraged it, had continued unaltered.

Paragraph 3: Here Mill returns to the importance of the problem (IB). What are the new circumstances that require our problem to be re-thought? As some governments became more representative, the old adversary relationship disappeared. Now instead of limiting the government's power, there grew the idea of increasing it. "The nation did not need to be protected against its own will."

The reader should compare the difference between the "old" liberal who seeks to curb government power and the "new" liberal who seeks to increase it. Which people today ask for the government to control social security, Medicare, welfare, wages and prices? Can the same government avoid fraud in public programs without resort to illegal wiretaps for example? Are we making contradictory demands?

4. But, in political and philosophical theories, as well as in persons, success discloses faults and infirmities which failure might have concealed from observation. The notion, that the people have no need to limit their power over themselves, might seem axiomatic, when popular government was a thing only dreamed about, or read of as having existed at some distant period of the past. Neither was that notion necessarily disturbed by such temporary aberrations as those of the French Revolution, the worst of which were the work of an usurping few, and which, in any case, belonged, not to the permanent working of popular institutions, but to a sudden and convulsive outbreak against monarchical and aristocratic despotism. In time, however, a democratic republic came to occupy a large portion of the earth's surface, and made itself felt as one of the most powerful members of the community of nations; and elective and responsible government became subject to the observations and criticisms which wait upon a great existing fact. It was now perceived that such phrases as "self-government," and "the power of the people over themselves," do not express the true state of the case. The "people" who exercise the power, are not always the same people with those over whom it is exercised; and the "self-government" spoken of, is not the government of each by himself, but of each by all the rest. The will of the people, moreover, practically means, the will of the most

numerous or the most active *part* of the people; the majority, or those who succeed in making themselves accepted as the majority: the people, consequently, *may* desire to oppress a part of their number; and precautions are as much needed against this, as against any other abuse of power. The limitation, therefore, of the power of government over individuals, loses none of its importance when the holders of power are regularly accountable to the community, that is, to the strongest party therein. This view of things, recommending itself equally to the intelligence of thinkers and to the inclination of those important classes in European society to whose real or supposed interests democracy is adverse, has had no difficulty in establishing itself; and in political speculations "the tyranny of the majority" is now generally included among the evils against which society requires to be on its guard.

Paragraph 4: Mill continues to discuss IB. The concept he introduces to explain the new circumstances for the old problem is "the tyranny of the majority." *What is the tyranny of the majority?*

(1) the oppression of the minority or minorities by the majority;

(2) the oppression of minorities by a minority which is the "most active part of the people," that is, an active minority that speaks or claims to speak on behalf of the "people."

Does the tyranny of the majority exist? What is the position of blacks in a predominantly white society? What is the position of Catholics in Protestant Northern Ireland? What is the position of Jews in a Moslem country such as Iraq, or vice versa? Do these tyrannies exist because some groups are more immoral than others, or because they are majorities? Mill borrowed the expression "tyranny of the majority" from Alexis de Tocqueville (1805-59), a French liberal politician and writer, who used it in his classic work *Democracy in America* (1835). The original meaning of the term *democracy,* in Greek, was mob rule.

5. Like other tyrannies, the tyranny of the majority was at first, and is still vulgarly, held in dread, chiefly as operating through the acts of the public authorities. But reflecting persons perceived that when society is itself the tyrant—society collectively, over the separate individuals who compose it—its means of tyrannizing are not restricted to the acts which it may do by the hands of its political functionaries. Society can and does execute its own mandates: and if it issues wrong mandates instead of right, or any mandates at all in things with which it ought not to meddle, it practices a social tyranny more formidable than many kinds of political oppression, since, though not usually upheld by such extreme penalities, it leaves fewer means of escape, penetrating much more deeply into the details of life, and enslaving the soul itself. Protection, therefore, against the tyranny of the magistrate is not enough: there needs protection also against the tyranny of the prevailing opinion and feeling; against the tendency of society to impose, by other means than civil penalities, its own ideas and practices as rules of conduct on those who dissent from them; to fetter the development, and, if possible, prevent the formation, of any individuality not in harmony with its ways, and compel all characters to fashion themselves upon the model of its own. There is a limit to the legitimate interference of collective opinion with individual independence: and to find that limit, and maintain it against encroachment, is as indispensable to a good condition of human affairs, as protection against political despotism.

Paragraph 5: Mill further defines the problem. The real culprit is not the government but society. "Social tyranny" is "more formidable than many kinds of political oppression." Why? Can you think of a serious social problem recently solved through political means?

Mill begins to approach the solution of his problem by formulating the question (IA) more clearly; notice the importance of "society" as opposed to government in Mill's formulation.

"There is a limit to the legitimate interference of collective opinion with individual independence: and to find that limit, and maintain it against encroachment, is as indispensable to a good condition of human affairs as protection against political despotism."

6. But though this proposition is not likely to be contested in general terms, the practical question, where to place the limit—how to make the fitting adjustment between individual independence and social control is a subject on which nearly everything remains to be done. All that makes existence valuable to any one, depends on the enforcement of restraints upon the actions of other people. Some rules of conduct, therefore, must be imposed, by law in the first place, and by opinion on many things which are not fit subjects for the operation of law. What these rules should be, is the principal question in human affairs; but if we except a few of the most obvious cases, it is one of those which least progress has been made in resolving. No two ages, and scarcely any two countries, have decided it alike; and the decision of one age or country is a wonder to another. Yet the people of any given age and country no more suspect any difficulty in it, than if it were a subject on which mankind had always been agreed. The rules which obtain among themselves appear to them self-evident and self-justifying. This all but universal illusion is one of the examples of the magical influence of custom, which is not only, as the proverb says, a second nature, but is continually mistaken for the first. The effect of custom, in preventing any misgiving respecting the rules of conduct which mankind impose on one another, is all the more complete because the subject is one on which it is not generally considered necessary that reasons should be given, either by one person to others, or by each to himself. People are accustomed to believe, and have been encouraged in the belief by some who aspire to the character of philosophers, that their feelings, on subjects of this nature, are better than reasons, and render reasons unnecessary. The practical prin-

ciple which guides them to their opinions on the regulation of human conduct, is the feeling in each person's
mind that everybody should be required to act as he, and
those with whom he sympathizes, would like them to act.
No one, indeed, acknowledges to himself that his standard of judgment is his own liking; but an opinion on a
point of conduct, not supported by reasons, can only
count as one person's preference; and if the reasons, when
given, are a mere appeal to a similar preference felt by
other people, it is still only many people's liking instead
of one. To an ordinary man, however, his own preference,
thus supported, is not only a perfectly satisfactory reason,
but the only one he generally has for any of his notions of
morality, taste, or propriety, which are not expressly written in his religious creed; and his chief guide in the interpretation even of that. Men's opinions, accordingly, on
what is laudable or blameable, are affected by all the
multifarious causes which influences their wishes in regard to the conduct of others, and which are as numerous
as those which determine their wishes on any other subject. Sometimes their reason—at other times their preju-
dices or superstitions; often their social affections, not
seldom their antisocial ones, their envy or jealousy, their
arrogance or contemptuousness: but most commonly,
their desires or fears for themselves—their legitimate or
illegitimate self-interest. Wherever there is an ascendant
class, a large portion of the morality of the country ema-
nates from its class interests, and its feelings of class
superiority. The morality between Spartans and Helots,
between planters and negroes, between princes and subjects, between nobles and roturiers, between men and
women, has been for the most part the creation of these
class interests and feelings; and the sentiments thus gene-
rated, react in turn upon the moral feelings of the members of the ascendant class, in their relations among themselves. Where, on the other hand, a class, formerly ascendant, has lost its ascendancy, or where its ascendancy is
unpopular, the prevailing moral sentiments frequently
bear the impress of an impatient dislike of superiority.

Another grand determining principle of the rules of conduct, both in act and forebearance, which have been enforced by law or opinion, has been the servility of mankind towards the supposed preferences or aversions of their temporal masters, or of their gods. This servility, though essentially selfish, is not hyprocrisy; it gives rise to perfectly genuine sentiments of abhorrence; it made men burn magicians and heretics. Among so many baser influences, the general and obvious interests of society have of course had a share, and a large one, in the direction of the moral sentiments: less, however, as a matter of reason, and on their own account, than as a consequence of the sympathies and antipathies which grew out of them: and sympathies and antipathies which had little or nothing to do with the interests of society, have made themselves felt in the establishment of moralities with quite as great force.

Paragraph 6: Before offering his own answer, Mill considers the answer we already have or have operated with. These (IID) include:

      (a) custom
      (b) personal feelings
      (c) self-interest
      (d) religious prejudice.

Note Mill's mention of women and their subservient position to men in most societies. This is another instance of tyranny. Mill was one of the first to champion the liberation of women. His work *On the Subjection of Women* (written in 1861 and published in 1869) is still a classic. Mrs. Harriet Taylor undoubtedly influenced him on this issue, both before and after their marriage. Women are now fifty-two percent of the U.S. population. Will women's liberation eventually become a kind of tyranny?

    7. The likings and dislikings of society, or of some powerful portion of it, are thus the main thing which has practically determined the rules laid down for general observ-

ance, under the penalties of law or opinion. And in general, those who have been in advance of society in thought and feeling, have left this condition of things unassailed in principle, however they may have come into conflict with it in some of its details. They have occupied themselves rather in inquiring what things society ought to like or dislike, than in questioning whether its likings or dislikings should be a law to individuals. They preferred endeavoring to alter the feelings of mankind on the particular points on which they were themselves heretical, rather than make common cause in defense of freedom, with heretics generally. The only case in which the higher ground has been taken on principle and maintained with consistency, by any but an individual here and there, is that of religious belief: a case instructive in many ways, and not least so as forming a most striking instance of the fallibility of what is called the moral sense: for the *odium theologicum,* in a sincere bigot, is one of the most unequivocal cases of moral feeling. Those who first broke the yoke of what called itself the Universal Church, were in general as little willing to permit difference of religious opinion as that Church itself. But when the heat of the conflict was over, without giving a complete victory to any party, and each church or sect was reduced to limit its hopes to retaining possession of the ground it already occupied; minorities, seeing that they had no chance of becoming majorities, were under the necessity of pleading to those whom they could not convert, for permission to differ. It is accordingly on this battlefield, almost solely, that the rights of the individual against society have been asserted on broad grounds of principle, and the claim of society to exercise authority over dissentients, openly controverted. The great writers to whom the world owes what religious liberty it possesses, have mostly asserted freedom of conscience as an indefeasible right, and denied absolutely that a human being is accountable to others for his religious belief. Yet so natural to mankind is intolerance in whatever they really care about, that religious freedom has hardly anywhere been practically realized, except where religious indifference, which dislikes to have its peace disturbed by theological quarrels, has added its weight to the scale. In the minds of almost all religious persons, even in the most tolerant countries, the duty of toleration is admitted with tacit reserves. One person will bear with dissent in matters of church government, but not of dogma; another can tolerate everybody, short of a Papist or an Unitarian, another, every one who believes in revealed religion; a few extend their charity a little further, but stop at the belief in a God and in a future state. Wherever the sentiment of the majority is still genuine and intense, it is found to have abated little of its claim to be obeyed.

8. In England, from the peculiar circumstances of our political history, though the yoke of opinion is perhaps heavier, that of law is lighter, than in most other countries of Europe; and there is considerable jealousy of direct interference, by the legislative or the executive power, with private conduct; not so much from any just regard for the independence of the individual, as from the still subsisting habit of looking on the government as representing an opposite interest to the public. The majority have not yet learnt to feel the power of the government their power, or its opinions their opinions. When they do so, individual liberty will probably be as much exposed to invasion from the government, as it already is from public opinion. But, as yet, there is a considerable amount of feeling ready to be called forth against any attempt of the law to control individuals in things in which they have not hitherto been accustomed to be controlled by it; and this with very little discrimination as to whether the matter is, or is not, within the legitimate sphere of legal control; insomuch that the feeling, highly salutary on the whole, is perhaps quite as often misplaced as well grounded in the particular instances of its application. There is, in fact, no recognized principle by which the propriety or or impropriety of government interference is customarily tested. People decide according to their personal preferences.

194

Some, whenever they see any good to be done, or evil to be remedied, would willingly instigate the government to undertake the business; while others prefer to bear almost any amount of social evil, rather than add one to the departments of human interests amenable to governmental control. And men range themselves on one or the other side in any particular case, according to this general direction of their sentiments; or according to the degree of interest which they feel in the particular thing which it is proposed that the government should do, or according to the belief they entertain that the government would, or would not, do it in the manner they prefer; but very rarely on account of any opinion to which they consistently adhere, as to what things are fit to be done by a government. And it seems to me that in consequence of this absence of rule or principle, one side is at present as often wrong as the other; the interference of government is, with about equal frequency improperly invoked and improperly condemned.

Paragraph 7 & 8: (IID): Mill has two objections to previous answers. First, (paragraph 7) past reformers have concentrated on substituting new dogma for old. Second, there has been (paragraph 8) a total "absence of rule or principle." That is, there has not been a consistent policy. Can you think of cases where our society has been too oppressive? Can you think of cases where our society has been too permissive? If a society can be both at the same time, how would you account for this possibility?

9. The object of this Essay is to assert one very simple principle, as entitled to govern absolutely the dealings of society with the individual in the way of compulsion and control, whether the means used by physical force in the form of legal penalities, or the moral coercion of public opinion. That principle is, that the sole end for which mankind are warranted, individually or collectively, in interfering with the liberty of action of any of their number, is self-protection. That the only purpose for which

power can be rightfully exercised over any member of a civilized community, against his will, is to prevent harm to others. His own good, either physical or moral, is not a sufficient warrant. He cannot rightfully be compelled to do or forbear because it will be better for him to do so, because it will make him happier, because, in the opinions of others, to do so would be wise, or even right. These are good reasons for remonstrating with him, or reasoning with him, or persuading him, or entreating him, but not for compelling him, or visiting him with any evil in case he do otherwise. To justify that, the conduct from which it is desired to deter him, must be calculated to produce evil to some one else. The only part of the conduct of any one, for which he is amenable to society, is that which concerns others. In the part which merely concerns himself, his independence or right, is absolute. Over himself, over his own body and mind, the individual is sovereign.

Paragraph 9: Mill gives his answer (IIA): "The sole end for which mankind are warranted . . . in interfering with the liberty of action of any of their number is self-protection . . . to prevent harm to others." The private area is defined by Mill as "the body and mind." Mill specifically excludes interfering when the private person's "own good, either physical or moral," is involved. This does not imply that we may not interfere with another's body when harm to others is at stake. Sufferers of contagious diseases are not at liberty to disregard their bodies.

Note as well that Mill does not advocate indifference to others in the private zone: "There are good reasons for remonstrating with him, or reasoning with him, or persuading him, or entreating him, but not for compelling him, or visiting him with any evil in case he do otherwise."

10. It is, perhaps, hardly necessary to say that this doctrine is meant to apply only to human beings in the maturity of their faculties. We are not speaking of children or of young persons below the age which the law may fix as

that of manhood or womanhood. Those who are still in a state to require being taken care of by others, must be protected against their own actions as well as against external injury. For the same reason, we may leave out of consideration those backward states of society in which the race itself may be considered as in its nonage. The early difficulties in the way of spontaneous progress are so great, that there is seldom any choice of means for overcoming them; and a ruler full of the spirit of improvement is warranted in the use of any expedients that will attain an end, perhaps otherwise unattainable. Despotism is a legitimate mode of government in dealing with barbarians, provided the end be their improvement, and the means justified by actually effecting that end. Liberty, as a principle has no application to any state of things anterior to the time when mankind have become capable of being improved by free and equal discussion. Until then, there is nothing for them but implicit obedience to an Akbar or a Charlemagne, if they are so fortunate as to find one. But as soon as mankind have attained the capacity of being guided to their own improvement by conviction or persuasion (a period long since reached in all nations with whom we need here concern ourselves), compulsion, either in the direct form or in that of pains and penalties for non-compliance, is no longer admissible as a means to their own good, and justifiable only for the security of others.

Paragraph 10: Mill adds some qualifications to his answer (IIA). His theory only applies to *rational individuals.* Such individuals are defined as those with "the capacity of being guided to their own improvement by conviction or persuasion," that is, those who are "capable of being improved by free and equal discussion." According to Mill this excludes: (1) children and (2) backward states of society. It follows that "despotism is a legitimate mode of government in dealing with barbarians, provided the end be their improvement and the means justified by actually effecting that end."

It should be clear that Mill views both of these states as temporary, not permanent or inherent. Mill was very much concerned with the problems of colonialism. He and his father, by their employment in the East India Company, had great experience with the ruling of India. For J. S. Mill's views on this subject consult his *Considerations on Representative Government* (1861), chapter eighteen. There Mill debunks the economic interpretation of empires, points out that in "the subject community also there are oppressors and oppressed," and claims that no one really knows yet how to establish a benevolent and temporary despotism. Those who are concerned with introducing democracy into other countries may well ponder this difficulty.

11. It is proper to state that I forgo any advantage which could be derived to my argument from the idea of abstract right, as a thing independent of utility. I regard utility as the ultimate appeal on all ethical questions; but it must be utility in the largest sense, grounded on the permanent interests of man as a progressive being. Those interests, I contend, authorize the subjection of individual spontaneity to external control, only in respect to those actions of each, which concern the interest of other people. If any one does an act hurtful to others, there is a *primâ facie* case for punishing him, by law, or, where legal penalities are not safely applicable, by general disapprobation. There are also many positive acts for the benefit of others, which he may rightfully be compelled to perform; such as, to give evidence in a court of justice; to bear his fair share in the common defense, or in any other joint work necessary to the interest of the society of which he enjoys the protection; and to perform certain acts of individual beneficence, such as saving a fellow creature's life, or interposing to protect the defenseless against ill-usage, things which whenever it is obviously a man's duty to do, he may rightfully be made responsible to society for not doing. A person may cause evil to others not only by his actions but by his inaction, and in either case he is justly accountable to them for the injury.

The latter case, it is true, requires a much more cautious exercise of compulsion than the former. To make any one answerable for doing evil to others, is the rule; to make him answerable for not preventing evil, is, comparatively speaking, the exception. Yet there are many cases clear enough and grave enough to justify that exception. In all things which regard the external relations of the individual, he is *de jure* amenable to those whose interests are concerned, and if need be, to society as their protector. There are often good reasons for not holding him to the responsibility; but these reasons must arise from the special expediencies of the case: either because it is a kind of case in which he is on the whole likely to act better, when left to his own discretion, than when controlled in any way in which society have it in their power to control him; or because the attempt to exercise control would produce other evils, greater than those which it would prevent. When such reasons as these preclude the enforcement of responsibility the conscience of the agent himself should step into the vacant judgment seat, and protect those interests of others which have no external protection; judging himself all the more rigidly, because the case does not admit of his being made accountable to the judgment of his fellow-creatures.

Paragraph 11: Mill turns now to the defense of his answer (IIB). First, Mill avoids appealing to "rights." Why? To begin with, since there are so many rights, many of which come into conflict in specific cases, we would be left without a guiding principle in cases of conflict. Second, the theory of rights presupposes a clear conception of an unchanging and fixed human nature. Against this, Mill argues for the notion of man "as a progressive being." This will become clearer in other chapters of the essay, but Mill does not believe in a fixed human nature. His perspective is evolutionary (man grows) but not teleological; that is, we are not growing in a predetermined direction.

Let us return to the first argument, namely that rights are inadequate. Mill suggests that we need a system in which we have a principle of ultimate appeal in case of conflict. This he proposes to find in the appeal to *utility*. Mill is known as a utilitarian, and he wrote a famous work, entitled *Utilitarianism* (1863). We cannot go into that complex work here, but it is only necessary to point out that Mill defended the principle of utility because it could resolve disputes when lower level principles conflicted. His example in *On Liberty* for the application of his answer is two-tiered: First we ask, "Is an act hurtful to others?" Next we ask, "Would preventing that hurtful act produce other evils, greater than those which it would prevent?" Recall the case of Prohibition.

12. But there is a sphere of action in which society, as distinguished from the individual, has, if any, only an indirect interest; comprehending all that portion of a person's life and conduct which affects only himself, or if it also affects others, only with their free, voluntary, and undeceived consent and participation. When I say only himself, I mean directly, and in the first instance: for whatever affects himself, may affect others *through* himself; and the objection which may be grounded on this contingency, will receive consideration in the sequel. This, then, is the appropriate region of human liberty. It comprises, first, the inward domain of consciousness; demanding liberty of conscience, in the most comprehensive sense; liberty of thought and feeling; absolute freedom of opinion and sentiment on all subjects, practical or speculative, scientific, moral, or theological. The liberty of expressing and publishing opinions may seem to fall under a different principle, since it belongs to that part of the conduct of an individual which concerns other people; but, being almost of as much importance as the liberty of thought, itself, and resting in great part on the same reasons, is practically inseparable from it. Secondly, the principle requires liberty of tastes and pursuits; of framing the plan of our life to suit our own character; of doing as we like, subject to such consequences as may follow: without impediment from our fellow-creatures, so long as what we do does not harm them, even though they should

think our conduct foolish, perverse, or wrong. Thirdly, from this liberty of each individual, follows the liberty, within the same limits, of combination among individuals; freedom to unite, for any purpose not involving harm to others; the persons combining being supposed to be of full age, and not forced or deceived.

Paragraph 12: in this paragraph Mill does two things. First, he further clarifies what his answer implies. Second, he considers objections to his theory.

The zone of privacy has already been established in paragraph 9 as the mind and body. This means specifically: (1) freedom of thought and expression (further elaborated in chapter 2); (2) freedom to choose one's life style (further elaborated in chapter 3); and (3) freedom for "combination among individuals" to do the same again with the provision that it not "harm others."

The reader should note how carefully Mill's first chapter sets the stage for his later chapters. He was apparently always asking himself how his reader would respond to what he had just said. He must have also worked with an outline and asked himself, "Why write this rather than that; why put this paragraph here rather than there?"

We come now to IID. What objection against his theory does Mill consider? He considers something that has become the standard reply: *Is there any such thing as an action which only concerns the individual?* He readily admits that "whatever affects himself may affect others through himself." His reply is to postpone a direct answer to this objection. He takes it up at length in chapter 4. See the next paragraphy.

13. No society in which these liberties are not, on the whole, respected, is free, whatever may be its form of government; and none is completely free in which they do not exist absolute and unqualified. The only freedom which deserves the name, is that of pursuing our own good in our own way, so long as we do not attempt to deprive others of theirs, or impede their efforts to obtain it. Each

is the proper guardian of his own health, whether bodily,
or mental and spiritual. Mankind are greater gainers by
suffering each other to live as seems good to themselves,
than by compelling each to live as seems good to the rest.

Paragraph 13: In this paragraph Mill does indicate what his
ultimate answer will be and in so doing reveals more clearly what
his facts and assumptions are (IIC). He says, "Mankind are greater gainers by suffering each other to live as seems good to themselves than by compelling each to live as seems good to the rest."
He goes no further here, but in chapter 3 he tries to show,
through *factual historical examples,* that societies have always
progressed because some individuals were courageous enough to
be different.

The *assumption* behind his argument, as seen in paragraph
11, is that man does not have a fixed nature. There will always be
new conditions to be faced requiring new responses, and as long
as the race is free to develop alternatives, it is likely to survive. To
assume that man has a fixed nature, or that no new conditions
will have to be faced, are assumptions of infallible knowledge on
the part of Mill's opponents. He will demolish the assumption of
infallibility in chapter 2.

14. Though this doctrine is anything but new, and, to some
persons, may have the air of a truism, there is no doctrine
which stands more directly opposed to the general tendency of existing opinion and practice. Society has ex-
pended fully as much effort in the attempt (according to
its lights) to compel people to conform to its notions of
personal, as of social excellence. The ancient common-
wealths thought themselves entitled to practice, and the
ancient philosophers countenanced, the regulation of
every part of private conduct by public authority, on the
ground that the State had a deep interest in the whole
bodily and mental discipline of every one of its citizens; a
mode of thinking which may have been admissible in
small republics surrounded by powerful enemies, in constant peril of being subverted to foreign attack or internal

commotion, and to which even a short interval of relaxed energy and self-command might so easily be fatal, that they could not afford to wait for the salutary permanent effects of freedom. In the modern world, the greater size of political communities, and above all, the separation between spiritual and temporal authority (which placed the direction of men's consciences in other hands than those which controlled their worldly affairs), prevented so great an interference by law in the details of private life; but the engines of moral repression have been wielded more strenuously against divergence from the reigning opinion in self-regarding, than even in social matters; religion, the most powerful of the elements which have entered into the formulation of moral feeling, having almost always been governed either by the ambition of a hierarchy, seeking control over every department of human conduct, or by the spirit of Puritanism. And some of those modern reformers who have placed themselves in strongest opposition to the religions of the past, have been noway behind either churches or sects in their assertion of the right of spiritual domination: M. Comte, in particular, whose social system, as unfolded in his *Traité de Politique Positive,* aims at establishing (though by moral more than by legal appliances) a despotism of society over the individual, surpassing anything contemplated in the political ideal of the most rigid disciplinarian among the ancient philosophers.

Paragraph 14.: In this paragraph Mill considers the objection (IID) which would be raised by those who would formulate the problem differently (IIIA) and (IID). There are those who would argue that "the State" has "a deep interest in the whole bodily and mental discipline of every one of its citizens." Mill thinks of the individual as related to society the way a person may or may not be a member of a club. Presumably, individuals may choose and be chosen. His opponents have an *organic* conception of the individual and society. That is, they would argue that an individual is like a part of the body, a limb for example, and cannot survive or have a separate identity apart from social function. The reader must decide which of these alternatives is more plausible.

Mill attributes his opponents' views to the insecure conditions of ancient life, which no longer existed for him. Is this a correct account of why others have the organic view (IIIB)? Mill cites as an example the French thinker Comte (ID). Other examples not mentioned would be Marx, Hegel, and in England, T. H. Green.

15. Apart from the peculiar tenets of individual thinkers, there is also, in the world at large an increasing inclination to stretch unduly the powers of society over the individual, both by the force of opinion and even by that of legislation: and as the tendency of all the changes taking place in the world is to strengthen society, and diminish the power of the individual, this encroachment is not one of the evils which tend spontaneously to disappear, but, on the contrary, to grow more and more formidable. The disposition of mankind, whether as rulers or as fellow-citizens, to impose their own opinions and inclinations as a rule of conduct on others, is so energetically supported by some of the best and by some of the worst feelings incident to human nature, that it is hardly ever kept under restraint by anything but want of power; and as the power is not declining, but growing, unless a strong barrier of moral conviction can be raised against the mischief, we must expect, in the present circumstances of the world, to see it increase.

Paragraph 15: Mill repeats why the problem is important for his own time. Is it important for our time?

16. It will be convenient for the argument, if, instead of at once entering upon the general thesis, we confine ourselves in the first instance to a single branch of it, on which the principle here stated, is, if not fully, yet to a certain point, recognized by the current opinions. This one branch is the Liberty of Thought: from which it is impossible to separate the cognate liberty of speaking

and of writing. Although these liberties, to some considerable amount, form part of the political morality of all
countries which profess religious toleration and free institutions, the grounds, both philosophical and practical, on
which they rest, are perhaps not so familiar to the general
mind, nor so thoroughly appreciated by many even of
the leaders of opinion, as might have been expected.
Those grounds, when rightly understood, are of much
wider application than to only one division of the subject,
and a thorough consideration of this part of the question
will be found the best introduction to the remainder.
Those to whom nothing which I am about to say will be
new, may therefore, I hope, excuse me, if on a subject
which for now three centuries has been so often discussed,
I venture on one discussion more.

Paragraph 16: Mill ends this chapter by indicating what he
will do in the next chapter. He claims that he will take up the
issue of censorship and use it as an example; if you agree with
what he says about censorship, then he thinks you will agree with
his argument as a whole. "Those grounds, when rightly understood, are of much wider application."

Exercises

EXERCISE 1

Identify the fallacy or potential difficulties in each of the following statements. More than one answer is sometimes possible.

1. Drink Schaeffer! It's New York's largest-selling beer.
2. According to the *Congressional Record* of June 6, Mr. Smith is a Communist.
3. Since everything in the universe has a beginning, the universe as a whole must have a beginning.
4. Of course Jones is in favor of building more hospitals. He's a building contractor, isn't he?
5. Of course Senator Jackson is in favor of bigger defense spending. The economy of his state depends on it.
6. I am not inconsistent, I am a pragmatist.
7. The U.S. should never get involved with countries where French is spoken. Look at what happened in Vietnam, in Lebanon, and in Haiti!
8. I refuse to take the polygraph test because the very suggestion that I take such a test is an attack on my integrity.
9. How can you possibly attack the Head-Start program? It has been successful in providing jobs and stimulating the economy.
10. We have to make a deal with Mayor Daley. Even John Kennedy did it.
11. The FX 17 has to be a superior fighter plane to the FX 16.

206

12. God helps those who help themselves.
13. Everything is relative.
14. Our program has been successful. Ask those who participated in it.
15. Have you stopped beating your wife?
16. The jury will never believe a three-time loser.
17. Make him an offer he can't refuse.
18. Everyone is a product of his environment; so we cannot really blame criminals. The real culprits are the members of the establishment who made the environment.
19. Our country should never become involved in any war, because all wars offer too many opportunities for criminal and immoral behavior on the part of our own troops.
20. We are not establishing quotas, we are against quotas. We are merely setting goals that we think can be achieved by a good-faith effort within the allotted timetables. Naturally, the best way to show your good faith is to achieve the goal.
21. This is a recession and not a depression.
22. IQ tests are not reliable. They do not measure intelligence but measure only the ability to comprehend and manipulate symbols. Besides, no one knows what intelligence really is.
23. There are two major problems in our society: first, not enough people get their fair share; and second, our society is too materialistic.
24. Eskimos are not short. I know of one who is seven feet tall.
25. Women earn less money than men; so your wife must earn less than you do.
26. Women have traditionally been discriminated against. Now it is time for men to get a taste of their own medicine.
27. Some have accused my administration of failure. But I see it as a glass half full rather than as a glass half empty.
28. Plaintiff's attorney: "I know that the defendant's experts claim that he could not possibly be the father of my client's child, but experts have been known to be mistaken. Besides, he deserves to be punished for having sexual relations out of wedlock."

29. Instead of choosing between excellence and quotas, let us compromise: each group will be assigned a quota, but within each group there will be competition based upon excellence.

EXERCISE 2: INDUCTIVE FALLACIES

1. Without public support I could not succeed.
2. The Vietnam war is responsible for all those young men in the service who became addicts.
3. If I am not sabotaged by my enemies, my plan will succeed.
4. I am opposed to charging tuition for college. Without tuition-free education, I could never have become mayor of this city.
5. Minority-group members have criminal tendencies. Did you ever notice how many of them are in our jails?
6. It has been claimed that since the establishment of the special program in astrology, grades have become inflated. That is not so. The grade spread in the history and psychology departments, for example, have remained the same throughout this period.

EXERCISE 3: SYLLOGISMS

1. All invalid syllogisms violate one of our three rules, and this syllogism is valid. Consequently, this syllogism does not violate one of the three rules.
2. Wherever there is protest, there is injustice. Hence, there is no injustice in Spain, because there is no protest there.
3. No humanists are believers. Hence humanists cannot be moral because believers are not immoral.

ANSWERS TO EXERCISE 1

1. *Ad populum.*
2. Misguided appeal to authority. The *Congressional Record* contains any statement made by any congressman, whether it is substantiated or not.
3. Composition

4. *Ad hominem.*
5. *Ad hominem.*
6. Appeal to a higher truth.
7. Hasty generalization
8. *Ad hominem.* Abandon discussion.
9. Red herring; call for perfection; nothing but objections; appeal to self-interest, etc.
10. Appeal to precedent.
11. Higher numbers.
12. Circular argument.
13. Inconsistency.
14. Appeal to self-interest.
15. Complex question.
16. *Ad hominem.*
17. Appeal to force (*ad baculum*).
18. Inconsistency.
19. Red herring; appeal to pity.
20. Equivocation; creative thinking.
21. Equivocation.
22. Equivocation; inconsistency.
23. Inconsistency.
24. Composition.
25. Division.
26. Two wrongs make a right.
27. Figurative analogy; red herring.
28. Attack on expertise; red herring.
29. Golden mean.

ANSWERS TO EXERCISE 2

1. Affirming the consequent.
   If I do not have public support then I fail.
   I failed.
2. *Post hoc* or a violation of Mill's Methods.
3. Affirming the consequent.
4. *Post hoc* (at least twice).

5. Concomitant variation.
6. Misleading statistics.

ANSWERS TO EXERCISE 3

1. All syllogisms that do not violate one of our three rules are valid syllogisms.
   This syllogism is a valid syllogism.
   Therefore, this syllogism is a syllogism that does not violate one of our three rules.
   Invalid (middle term not distributed).
2. *Invalid* (term distributed in the conclusion but not in the major premise).
3. *Invalid* (two negative premises).

Suggestions

It is important that arguments be seen as a set of interlocking or related statements. It is also important that readers have that most elusive of all skills, namely, the ability to be critical of one's own argument. To these ends I would suggest the following: Choose a topic that is both current and controversial—the legalization if marijuana, abortion, "triage" with respect to the population explosion and world food supply, etc. Construct an argument in favor of or against one of these positions. Then, present objections to your own argument. Finally, refute these objections. In short, follow the pattern I have outlined in this book: presenting your case, attacking your case, and defending your case. You should also include consideration of nonverbal devices one might use.

My experience with this kind of assignment when given to students is that many fail to do an adequate job in attacking their own case. This is to be expected. I have devised the following techniques for circumventing this difficulty. One possibility is to take a poll at the *beginning* of the semester on current and controversial issues, a poll in which each student is required to state his opinion on at least one issue. Later, when I assign the project of constructing a grand argument, I require each student to defend the point of view that he is against. That is, he must initially present a case on behalf of the position to which he is not sympathetic. Since two-thirds of his work is to present and defend that position against his own cherished objections, this technique is very effective. A second possibiity is to have topics worked on in pairs, wherein one person presents a case and then defends it against objections made by someone who is personally committed to the opposing point of view.

This first suggestion could easily be a term project that the student works on all semester. This can be done out of class and should be done so as to encourage the student to gather as much outside material as possible. As a term project it will allow the student to incorporate all of the issues and techniques during the course of the semester.

Throughout this book I have maintained that much of informal logic involves arguments that are formally valid but that contain one or more premises that would not be accepted as true. That is, much of informal logic is concerned with unsound argumentation. There are two ways in which this insight may be conveyed. First, as I have indicated in Chapter Six, most, if not all, of the informal fallacies may be reconstructed as unsound arguments. Consider the so-called fallacy of affirming a disjunct:

> *Either* inflation must halt *or* there will be a depression.
> The President will halt inflation.
> _____
> *Therefore,* there will be no depression.

It is clear to most people that there can be other causes of a depression besides inflation; so it does not necessarily follow that halting inflation by *any* means will prevent a depression. One may represent this point by claiming that affirming a disjunct— an either/or statement followed by the affirmation of one of the two disjuncts—is not acceptable. Alternatively, one may reconstruct the argument so that it is a formally valid syllogism, but with one of its premises obviously false. I think this latter method is a much better way of improving sensitivity to arguments. For example: All cases of economic depression are caused by inflation.

> This is a time when there will be no inflation.
> _____
> Therefore, this is a time when there will be no depression.

Without denying the consequences of inflation, I think it will be clear by such a reconstruction that the first premise is unacceptable. This type of reconstruction has the added benefit of showing your sympathy with your opponent. You are literally giving him the benefit of the doubt by trying to make his argument formally valid, but at the same time exposing its weak premise or premises. I suggest that all the examples of traditional informal fallacies, such as composition, division, etc., be assigned to students or taken by the readers and simply reconstructed.

Books, newspapers, especially editorials, student newspapers, magazines, and even television are an infinite source of potential arguments to be reconstructed. I think that it is much better to choose current items of popular interest than to supply artificial examples. Nevertheless, I shall supply a few arguments in the form of condensed statements that I suggest be reconstructed in order to uncover the premises.

(1) Women compose 52 percent of the population. Women make up, however, only 36 percent of all college faculties. Therefore, women have been discriminated against.

(2) Jews compose 2 percent of the population as a whole. Our medical school has a quota that permits only 5 percent of the class to be composed of Jews. Since our quota exceeds the national average, we are not discriminating against Jews.

(3) Three individuals are discussing solutions to the poverty problem. X argues that poverty will no longer exist when each person has an income in excess of $10,000 a year. Y argues that poverty will no longer exist when all people have identical incomes. Z argues that poverty will no longer exist when people do not feel poor, regardless of income. Reconstruct the different major premise from which each participant in the discussion begins.

Index